Pacific Sea & Shore

Pacific Sea & Shore

Photography by Ray Atkeson
Text by Archie Satterfield

The Writing Works
Seattle, Washington

Library of Congress Cataloging in Publication Data

Atkeson, Ray.
Pacific sea & shore.

(Panorama collection; bk. 1)
1. Pacific coast (United States)—
Description and travel. 2. Hawaii—Description and
travel—1981- . 3. Seashore biology—Pacific coast
(United States) 4. Seashore biology—
Hawaii. I. Satterfield, Archie. II. Title.
III. Title: Pacific sea and shore. IV. Series.
F852.2.A84 1982 917.9'0946 82-10910
ISBN 0-916076-53-9

Manufactured in the United States
Published by: The Writing Works
417 East Pine Street
Seattle, Washington 98122
The Writing Works is part of the
Cone-Heiden Corporation Group
Library of Congress Catalog Card Number: 82-10910
ISBN 0-916076-53-9 (Writing Works)

Colorful starfish wander over the rocks
and shallow tide pools to attack their prey,
mussels, snails and other crustaceans.

Pacific Sea and Shore

Project Editor - Merle Dowd
Designer - Doug Rice
Color separations and color supervision by Color Control, Inc., Redmond, WA.
Printing by Cone-Heiden, Seattle, WA.
Case binding by Hiller Industries, Salt Lake City, UT.
Paper - Plainwell Kashmir, 100 lb. Gloss, Plainwell Paper Co., Inc.
Typestyle - Baskerville

Acknowledgments

MY appreciation of the Pacific Coast and Hawaiian Islands is the result of several factors—and artistic benefactors—that began when I served aboard a ship during the Korean War that sailed out of San Diego. Through my Navy experience I was able to sail up and down the Pacific Coast with stops in Los Angeles, Monterey, San Francisco and Puget Sound. Nine indolent months were spent in the Hawaiian Islands and six months in the Marshall Island atolls of Eniwetok, Kwajalein and Bikini. Although it would be another two decades before I sailed on another ship on the Pacific, those four years aboard a Navy ship were engraved in my memory.

Although I have never had any pretensions of being a naturalist, an oceanographer or biologist, still my occupation as a newspaper reporter and editor in Seaside, Oregon, Longview, Washington, and later on Seattle's two major daily newspapers were instrumental in getting me to the coast frequently and often in the company of men and women whose lives were devoted to the study of the shore.

Since my arrival in the Northwest in 1959, I had always heard one name mentioned every time photographs of the region were the topic of conversations. That name was Ray Atkeson, and he had been in the Northwest as long as I had been alive. Frankly, I was in awe of his talent and reputation, and it never occurred to me when I was getting started as a writer that one day I would not only be working with Ray on books, but that I would also consider him one of my most valued friends. It was a very important day in my life, and certainly in my career, when Ray called to ask if I would write the text for one of his books. This is the fourth book we have produced together, and we both hope there will be many more to come.

Many other people have helped me at various stages of my career, and I would like to single out one more: Max Schafer, Sr., who was publisher of the *Seaside Signal* and my first employer. His enthusiasm and interest in the Pacific Coast were contagious, and most of my interest in the subject can be traced back to the year I worked for him as a newspaper editor-reporter.

Another person who has been of more help to my coastal education than he might suspect is Frank Rotta, director of public relations for Winnebago Industries. Twice I accepted assignments that involved considerable long-distance travel along the coast, once from Seattle to San Diego, and Frank graciously loaned me a motorhome in each instance. The prospect of making those trips with young children, packing and unpacking each morning and evening in motel rooms, was almost enough to make me turn down the assignment. But Frank came to the rescue each time.

Archie Satterfield

YOU waken slowly and the first sound you hear is the muffled roar of the surf that lulled you into a sleep so deep it was almost a hypnotic trance. When you awaken before first light you are filled with a vague restlessness. You want to be outside, at the edge of the continent where sea and land meet. You want to see again what you saw yesterday and what living creatures have seen for centuries beyond counting.

Where sea and shore meet along the Pacific Coast is to many the most dramatic place in the universe. It is a distinct boundary between the frontiers of the land and the sea. Some living creatures are able to live their entire lives on this frontier, but man, with all his knowledge and trinkets and toys, cannot. The more man examines and explores this frontier, the more mysterious it becomes.

As you walk along the shoreline in first light, or stand on a promontory watching this endless, repetitious interplay of land and sea, you cannot help but wonder what the first man to stand on this spot thought. Nor can you avoid marveling at the tenacity of the first creature to venture beyond the line of the surf, if only for an instant, before trying and trying again until it could survive there a few minutes, then a few hours until the next tide came, and finally indefinitely.

We will never know why these creatures, perhaps our genetic forebears, left the sea for land. Perhaps it is something as simple to say but impossible to understand as "Nature abhors a vacuum," and land before living creatures was a vacuum.

These are the kinds of elliptical, inconclusive thoughts that come with dawn on the coast. When the sun rises over the headlands and you can see the whole expanse of sea, beach and land, the mysteries of those pre-dawn moments are not forgotten; they are pushed aside by more sensual stimuli, including the thought of breakfast.

IF it is true that all living creatures originated in the sea, and that in the very beginning of life on this planet there was only the sea, then this might help explain part of the attraction the sea exerts upon us. This pull toward the seashore is almost as strong among some people as the moon's pull on the ocean itself.

Or perhaps it is nothing more mysterious than a visual "pull" by the incredible beauty found along the Pacific Coast of America. History may repeat itself, in part because mankind's experiences are both limited and cyclical. But the coastal scenery has no such limits. The two basic elements of sea and clouds are without such limitations, and no two days, no two scenes will ever be the same.

WHEN describing the interaction between sea and land, writers are given to calling it a continual struggle between these elements. How else to explain a storm wave thundering against an offshore rock which thousands or millions of years ago was part of the mainland? Rampart Rock on the Oregon Coast is one of the thousands of such offshore pinnacles which receive the sea's assaults daily, the erosion so minute that it hardly changes from generation to generation. Yet the erosion is real. One day the rock will exist only as part of the sand on the beach. Perhaps during our lifetime it will be undercut so deeply that we will go down to the beach one morning after a particularly severe storm and it will be lying on its side, a giant finally toppled by the sea.

VISITORS to the Pacific Coast of America are given a visual treat that few other coastlines in the world can offer. Much of this coastline is in public ownership, particularly in Oregon. The state's ownership of the shoreline came about almost as an accident. In the early years of settlement when New England was already old by American standards, the coastline had no value to residents. It was too rough for use as ports for sailing vessels, and few of the rivers entering the sea offered safe harbors. The land between these few harbors had no value at all. The state acquired most of the coastline and used as much as possible for pioneer trails, low-tide routes between settlements or farms. When highways were finally carved through the nearby forests and across the wild headlands, the state kept ownership of the coastline and created a large number of parks, such as this one at Rocky Creek.

ANOTHER state park that has been a haven for photographers and painters is Ecola State Park near the picturesque town of Cannon Beach, Oregon. Here the scenery is always different, always spectacular. It was here that Lewis and Clark visited enroute to see a beached whale at Cannon Beach. A trail leads from Ecola State Park north to Seaside past Indian Beach and over Tillamook Head with its panoramic views of the ocean and the Tillamook Rock Lighthouse a short distance offshore on a large pinnacle. The lighthouse has long been abandoned, and on certain days of the spring and fall, the setting sun casts a ghostly glint off the lighthouse glass that can be seen in Cannon Beach.

ALTHOUGH you know that many other visitors to the coast have walked in the same places you do, still these beach strolls give you a sense of discovery. There are parts of the Pacific Coast with little more than sandy beaches and rolling dunes stretching to the east, but it is the coastline with rocks and headlands and bays and smaller beaches that attracts most people. Here, sometimes hundreds of feet from the low-tide line, you will find tiny pools abandoned by the sea until the next high tide. These pools often create stunning reflections and house a variety of tidal zone creatures, such as crabs, mussels, starfish, barnacles and other life that lives along the shore.

Some of the pools are created by wave action swirling around a rock, or fresh water flowing from a nearby spring or stream into the sea, such as this one on Crescent Beach at Ecola State Park, Oregon.

Others are created around giant basaltic spires isolated by erosion from the rest of the mainland, such as that shown on the next page at Bandon, Oregon.

STAND for a few minutes, or even hours, at one spot along the shoreline, and you will be astonished at the number of changes you will see in the same scene. If clouds are in the sky, the entire composition of the scene will change constantly. Sometimes you will be aware only of the shoreline, and other times you will find yourself looking only at the cloud formations. The sun breaking through the cloud cover will emphasize some offshore rocks while leaving others dimly lit. The ebb and flow of the tide will change the entire character of shoreline. Although you may not be aware of the tide in the first few moments of beach watching, you must not permit yourself to become stranded around a point or on a rock that one hour is connected to the mainland and the next is a diminishing island. A beach you stood on early in the morning may not exist by noon. And a rather ordinary looking stretch of surf can become a maze of fascinating tidepools by mid-afternoon. *Overleaf.*

FOG is a necessity for your shoreline experience, and it has as many faces as a good character actor. In some stretches of coastline, particularly in northern California, it is a constant element. One can stand above the Big Sur coast, for example, in total sunlight and be unable to see the ocean directly below. Some visitors to this coast amuse themselves by standing on a cliff over the ocean with the strong morning sun casting their shadow onto the thick fog below. Here they dance, create semaphoric languages and contort their bodies while watching their shadows on the fog below.

Fog is a fact of coastal life. It changes colors with the quality of the sunlight above it. The sun throws streamers of light through it. It ranges from a brilliant rose to dull gray to the spectrum of rainbows. It creates fringes as it enters the forests along the coast, and sometimes permits the tips of offshore rocks to stand above the cool, moist cloud and catch the warm sunlight.

SHORELINE monoliths such as Haystack Rock at Cannon Beach in Oregon become symbols for entire areas along coastlines, particularly when they are approachable during low-tide periods. Then you can walk out to them and explore them before the next tide comes in to isolate them again. In this sense, they take on two identities, one rather mysterious when they cannot be approached, and another when only a walk over damp sand is required to clamber around them. Nearly all offshore rocks and seastacks along the Pacific coast are under federal management and are dedicated as bird refuges, making it illegal to climb on them. Since they are dangerous places to visit due to the danger of being stranded on them by incoming tides, and they are usually composed of "rotten" rock that crumbles off to the touch, the government's declaring them off limits to people is also for safety.

THESE offshore rocks so common on our coastline often were made by lava flows during the creation of the western shoreline, visible evidence of the so-called "Ring of Fire" that lines the Pacific Coast from Baja California north to Alaska and back down through the Aleutian Islands to Japan and Indonesia. These lava flows created many of the shelves and pinnacles along the coast as well as the Coast Range itself. The major difference is that the lava flows along the shore are kept swept clean of soil by the surf, and vegetation never has an opportunity to conceal the basic structure of the land. This unusual mile-long dike of lava provides a surf barrier at Seal Rocks State Park in Oregon.

SOMETIMES in the morning a strong east wind will blow down the mountains and out to sea against a heavy surf that was built up by a storm thousands of miles at sea. When these two opposing forces meet along the shoreline, the results can be spectacular examples of spindrift with the tops of the giant waves being ripped off by the wind and flung back to sea. If this occurs in sunny weather, you can expect to see a variety of colors appear in the spindrift, sometimes rainbows that appear, shimmer briefly, then disappear.

ON calmer seas the spindrift isn't so spectacular and the effect is more subtle, as though the wind were simply flattening out the surf before it reaches the shore. Under normal conditions with no storms in the area, the winds adopt a regularity much like a living thing breathing in and out once each day. In many areas the morning sea breezes blow inland, as the land heats faster than the ocean surface. During the night the land usually cools faster than the ocean surface, the process is reversed, and the wind blows out to sea. These are usually local winds only and only faintly related to the larger global weather patterns that are so complex that no meteorologist can make totally correct weather predictions. These localized winds usually give us breezes in the morning and evening and calm in the middle of the day.

MORNING along the Pacific Coast tends to offer more subtle, gentle scenery since it does not cast shadows between us and the sea. However, toward the end of the day the shadows begin appearing as the sun falls behind sea stacks and headlands, and the colors frequently deepen toward the primary colors in the spectrum. Deep blacks begin appearing as the rocks become silhouettes, the water a shimmering yellow or gold, and the sky a red with the yellow ball of the sun slowly losing its white-hot fire and becoming darker shades of yellow and red.

EVENING is a special time on a sunny, calm beach. Tired from the day's activities and with thoughts of a leisurely dinner followed by another night of deep, hypnotic sleep with the eons-old sound of the surf the last thing you hear, you will find yourself content to spend those last hours of daylight perched on a rock or log simply letting the day disappear from sight.

The sounds of the surf are so soothing to us that many people use tape recordings of the surf sounds to help them fall asleep each night; some people take these recordings with them when they travel to help them fall asleep in strange places. It provides the psychological security of something familiar.

The surf's primeval qualities have also been used for lulling babies to sleep, treating the mentally disturbed and a host of other relaxing uses. It is possible that this familiar sound is buried in our genes and harkens back across all those millions of years to the time when the first sea creature migrated to the shore and began life on land.

It has been said that the beach is the best babysitter of them all because children can amuse themselves on a beach for hours or days. Even workaholic adults visiting the shoreline find ways to occupy themselves without feeling that they have wasted an important part of their lives.

This must be part of the attraction the coast, particularly Hawaii, holds for vacationers. Once a man who is concerned about his business back home leaves his hotel room and goes for a stroll on the beach, he usually becomes totally engrossed with that simple act and nothing else. He will watch for seashells. He will become intrigued with the pattern of the waves and the way the weather conditions change the inland scenery. At night the hours have a way of disappearing when you sit on the balcony or other outdoor area with the sounds of the sea out there in the darkness.

If sound does not exist without an ear to hear it and give identity to the sound, then the shoreline can be said to exist only when each of us is standing on it. It does not need us, but it can be argued with conviction that we do need it. We are pulled toward it as surely as the tides respond to the gravitational pull of the moon. It is a part of us, both emotionally and physically. As the late, great Rachel Carson pointed out in her masterpiece, *The Sea Around Us,* "each of us carries in our veins the salty stream in which the elements of sodium, potassium and calcium are combined in almost the same proportions as in sea water."

Reduced to chemical formulas, our entire bodies are composed of the elements that are found in the sea. It is the mother of life and all living creatures on the earth are its children.

Those of us who are attracted to the sea and those who sail its surface and probe its depths in scuba gear or submarines have any number of ways to justify this temporary and carefully controlled returning. We use the same catch phrases common to mountain climbing and space exploration; to fulfill man's destiny; to seek out and explore new environments; to find new sources of food and minerals and oil. In many cases this may be true, but there still exists that vague yearning all living creatures feel for their birthplace. Those who spend more than a few hours of their lives beneath the surface of the sea usually feel strangely at peace while there and often dread returning to the reality of the shore.

The literature of science fiction contains frequent references to the ability of man, in some distant century, being able to return to the sea and live among the other creatures of the sea through the implantation of artificial gills or some such arrangement. These writers foresee the time when man will be able to control his metabolism as his distant relatives, the whales and dolphins and seals and other warm-blooded creatures do. Wishful thinking? Certainly. Impossible? Who can be sure?

The sea holds a tantalizing promise to man because like outer space it is familiar. It is visible, and we know only enough about it to hunger for more knowledge and experience in and about it.

Thus, when we gather at the beach to watch the sunset, awed into silence by the merging of two vital elements for all forms of life, we seldom think openly of the sun and the sea. Instead, we watch the shadows of the sea stacks growing longer and longer with the water a shimmering yellow or gold and the sky red with the glowing ball of the sun slowly losing its white-hot fire and becoming darker shades of yellow and gold before it suddenly drops into the darkness of the sea.

THE SEASHORE bursts with life, and the variety is the greatest you will find in any narrow strip of sea or land on the entire planet. Life wheels overhead, swims in the water, clings to the rocks in the tidal zone, crawls over the sand, grows roots down to the high-tide line and burrows into the earth.

A tidepool without some form of visible life is almost beyond imagining. A long sandy beach without telltale clam holes or at least sand fleas is impossible to visualize. If life should cease to exist along the shoreline, it will surely cease to exist elsewhere on this fragile planet.

The western coastline of America from Baja California to Point Barrow and westward to the Hawaiian Islands includes some of the most heavily used coastline in the world. Even though man treats the life along that seashore with less respect than most other living creatures, this dramatic conglomerate of life continues to replenish itself and thrive.

Where else in the world can you see so many species in one natural setting. There are birds, fishes, reptiles, amphibians, mollusks, crustaceans, bivalves, mammals, trees, ferns, moss, underbrush, vines and flowers. There are insects, microorganisms beyond counting, and there are seaweeds and...

To the visitor with a scientific bent, the seashore presents a laboratory in a dramatic setting. A casual visitor in search of sand and sun, on the other hand, will likely see only the birds overhead and the trees between the highway and the high-tide line.

Thus, another attraction the seashore holds! No matter your preferences and interests, you will find something there. Engineers marvel at the tenacity of barnacles and the great constructors—coral. What other creature on earth can build an island that will not be washed away in the next typhoon? A composer hears the highly ordered beat of the surf and the music of the wind. He knows that frequently not too far offshore in Maui the humpback whales are singing their infinitely lonely songs that they change each year. The architect, if he is totally honest with himself, knows that he can design buildings and neighborhoods and entire cities for the rest of his life and he will never accomplish the combination of form and function found in tiny tidepools. Man can never build a jetty as beautiful and functional as a coral reef, nor can any manmade island compare with the massive beauty of an offshore rock or a barren island abandoned by the mainland during eons past.

So we must be content to marvel at the work of creatures supposedly inferior to us. It is difficult to examine a stretch of shoreline carefully and still believe we are the most important creatures on earth. True, we can cause more changes than the other creatures because we use tools. But we cannot build a coral atoll, nor can we move back and forth between the sea and shore with the ease of many creatures of the tidepools.

We can, however, enjoy the intricate beauty—and the stark terror of the pursued—found in tidepools. In the business world and other forms of human endeavor that involve groups of people competing for power, we frequently compare our relationships to tidepools where only the strongest and the fittest survive. While this is an apt analogy for some situations, it is not quite accurate because we are competing against our own species rather than against other species.

Unfortunately, many stretches of shoreline along the Pacific Coast have been stripped of nearly all forms of life by our activities. We dump poisonous wastes into the sea (happily, this has declined markedly in the last decade), and we dredge and blast and fill over whole tidal zone communities when we build over the shore or create new anchorages for our boats and ships.

Gradually some of these barren stretches of shoreline have begun developing into new tidal communities. This is largely due to new laws enacted in each state to protect the shorelines from wanton destruction. California has its coastal protection legislation, as does the State of Washington. Oregon's coast has long been afforded a degree of protection through the public ownership of most of the coast. Hawaii has restricted shoreline development, more so on some islands than others.

Left alone for a sufficient time, life will eventually return to the tidal zone, as shown by artificial reefs built in some areas from old barges or stacks of worn-out truck and automobile tires. If the water is clean and living creatures can find a place to live, no area along the shore will be without life. Nature, we are fond of saying with some accuracy, abhors a vacuum.

SOME philosophers have said that if man grew flippers instead of fingers, we would never have achieved the technological prominence that keeps us feeling superior and makes us a danger to other living creatures. There remains the disquieting possibility that other mammals might be more intelligent than we are, but that those mammals are wise enough to remain free of possessions and technological toys. Until some cryptographer cracks the code that separates us from other mammals, we will never know. Typically, these intelligent mammals live in the sea. Although many have been slain to the edge of extinction by man, most species have managed to survive. The whales still cruise the coastline, seals wrap themselves in kelp for afternoon naps, and sea lions, such as these on the Oregon coast, maintain semipermanent residences in caves and secluded coves and offshore islands.

CERTAIN coastal scenes have entered our consciousness so deeply that we cannot conceive of a beach in those places without the identifying characteristic. In the Hawaiian Islands, scenes such as this at Kalapana Black Sands Beach state boldly that it is Hawaii. These rugged and virtually treeless shelves of cooled lava tell us bluntly how the islands were formed by volcanoes, and that the Island of Hawaii is the only one still growing from the lava that frequently oozes down from the Kilauea Crater and into the sea, adding more land to the island. Many centuries from now a new island will form southeast of the Island of Hawaii; it is already a seamount named Loihi. Geologists believe that the plates of the earth's crust have moved slowly toward the northwest in that area, and that a single reservoir of lava has created each of the Hawaiian Islands, beginning uncounted centuries ago with Midway and working downward in the chain past French Frigate Shoals and all the other atolls and islets to Kauai. Each of the earlier islands has eroded back into the sea.

THE trees along the western shore of the mainland north of Monterey Bay seldom become a symbol for an area. From Oregon northward it is rock formations that give a stronger identity to the area. However, the evergreen trees on the oceanfront strip of Olympic National Park of Washington have their own beauty as they struggle to survive in the shallow soil that has formed above high-tide line. Few plants are more tenacious than trees that establish themselves along the Olympic Peninsula coast. They are struck by frequent and wild winter storms, and the larger they grow, the more vulnerable they are to being toppled by these storms. Yet many live in precarious perches for decade after decade, often sending out roots like grappling hooks that dive back down into soil several feet away from the trunk. Life, once it occurs, does not think of defeat.

TO imagine a beach without seagulls is as difficult as thinking of a beach with no sounds of the sea. For seagulls are as much a sight and sound of the sea as the surf itself. Sometimes when we feel trapped by life, our dreams are of flying, and in those dreams we dive and soar and turn, feeling no wind in our faces, no sensation of falling, no fear of crashing into the rocks below or flying too high toward the sun. This surely explains part of the attraction we feel for seagulls. We see them riding out storms with no apparent concern. We see them tumbling about through apparent exuberance. We see them sitting on rocks with the surf spray cascading over them. We see them standing on the rail of our hotel lanai as though we did not exist. It is no wonder that Richard Bach did not choose an albatross or an owl or a hawk or crow for his hero in *Jonathan Livingston Seagull.* No other bird seems to possess that same blend of buffoon, statesman, dancer and singer.

EVEN when life has left a being of the shore, its skeleton can retain a dignity and even take on a new personality. A stump is a mutilated tree, to judge one with total objectivity. A stump standing in an open meadow where once a forest stood, perhaps rotting in the middle and with ferns or brush growing in the dark puddle of water it collects, is not quite the same thing as a stump that has been uprooted, picked up by a flood and taken down a river and out to sea. This stump has artistic merit. It eventually washes up on shore where it is blasted by wind-driven sand, bleached in the sun, gnawed at by fleas and slugs and snails until it becomes a complex piece of monolithic art.

IT is doubtful that a painter, even one specializing in photo-realistic art, could ever create a stump on canvas to match any selected at random on the shore. Who could capture the many, many shades of gray and silver? Who could design all the whirls of grain that do not look possible for a plant to create, yet are absolutely natural? How could an artist be expected to choose the proper way to place a stump on the beach so that its colors and roots and knobs make it look as though it always belonged where it now stands? True, a stump is the bottom of a dead tree, but loosen the grip on your imagination, and it becomes almost anything you want it to be. If you don't believe this, ask the next child who walks by what it looks like.

PUTTING natural beauty, artistic impressions and variations of ink-blot tests aside, consider how many houses or even towns could be built from the driftwood that finds its way to the beaches. Where it is permitted, residents of coastal communities have an excellent supply of firewood, and sometimes building materials, simply by driving to the beach with a truck. Using driftwood in fireplaces has its drawbacks, however; the sea water and salts trapped in the pores of driftwood often cause a series of minor explosions that in a winter or two can wreck a masonry fireplace.

Driftwood poses another hazard, a potentially fatal one: It can and has killed people climbing on logs when the surf is lapping at the jumble of logs stacked along the beach. One should stay well clear of logs when the surf is hitting them because the enormous power of a wave can flip logs around as casually as a majorette flings her baton skyward. *Overleaf.*

WHEN you stand in a coastal forest, you can't always distinguish between the sound of a wind coming through the trees and the sound of the surf in the distance. And during a heavy wind it is possible to walk through a coastal forest, such as this one in Oregon, and be virtually at the water's edge before realizing you have reached land's end. Forests, with their maze of spruce and hemlock and fir towering above and a thick carpet of salal, rhododendron and azaleas, all grow as close to the sea as they dare.

ALL jungles are not in the tropical climates, as evidenced by the famed rain forest of the Olympic Peninsula in Washington. Here, in areas protected from the violent winds of storms blowing in from the sea, rain and fog are almost a constant. Trees sprout, live and die, then fall to the earth to become nurse logs for the next generation of forest life. The forest floor is so nourished by the rain and decaying plants that a thick carpet of life covers the ground.

BECAUSE the sun is born in the east and dies in the west, because the Old World looked to the west for the New World, because the American West offered the last opportunity for American democracy in its purest form, because daylight ends where our recent ancestors' hopes of a new life lay, the West Coast is a barrier to those fading dreams and superstitions recorded on crumbling papers in world-weary Europe. Few Americans found what they were searching for when they reached this final edge. Many who came during the Dust Bowl era and the boom years of World War II have now gone back to their birthplace, the urge to move on forgotten in favor of the urge to belong. John Steinbeck's masterpiece, *The Red Pony,* tells of the westering urge buried in the genes of the old wagonmasters who led the pioneers across the plains and mountains and deserts to the Promised Land of California. But the promised land wasn't there. And the West ended there, leaving a group of disappointed old men standing on the shoreline with no more west to conquer.

THE Pacific Coast may be a disappointment to those who believe happiness lies at the end of a long journey, but the coast has never made anyone happy. It only makes it easier for people to *let* themselves be happy, to have a few moments throughout their lives to be relaxed, content. Scattered along the beaches of the shoreline are small enclaves that have been permitted to ignore change. Except for trails (and every living, moving creature, even man, should be permitted to make trails through the forest) places such as Cape Lookout State Park in Oregon have changed very little since the first forest grew, fell and regenerated itself. On early autumn afternoons such as this, with a light fog slipping in off the ocean, it is easy to forget everything except what your senses tell you.

SOME visitors to the shoreline want as few natural elements as possible; the sea and the sand are sufficient for them. Other elements, such as sculptured roots of a giant tree, only clutter the landscape for them. Thus, some would live nowhere else but the southern California coast where those two basic ingredients are dominant. The farther north one travels along the Pacific shore, the more complex, the more rugged the coastline becomes. The sea tends to be more placid in southern California and the tidal fluctuations less extreme. The farther north, the greater the tides and the more violent the winter storms.

THE trees that survive the weather along the Oregon and Washington coasts tend to develop their own strong identities and do not simply stand straight and tall with virtually identical branch systems like those deep in the protected forest. Trees with a view of the surf have allowed themselves to become contorted into strange shapes, such as this one that resembles a musical instrument, a lyre perhaps.

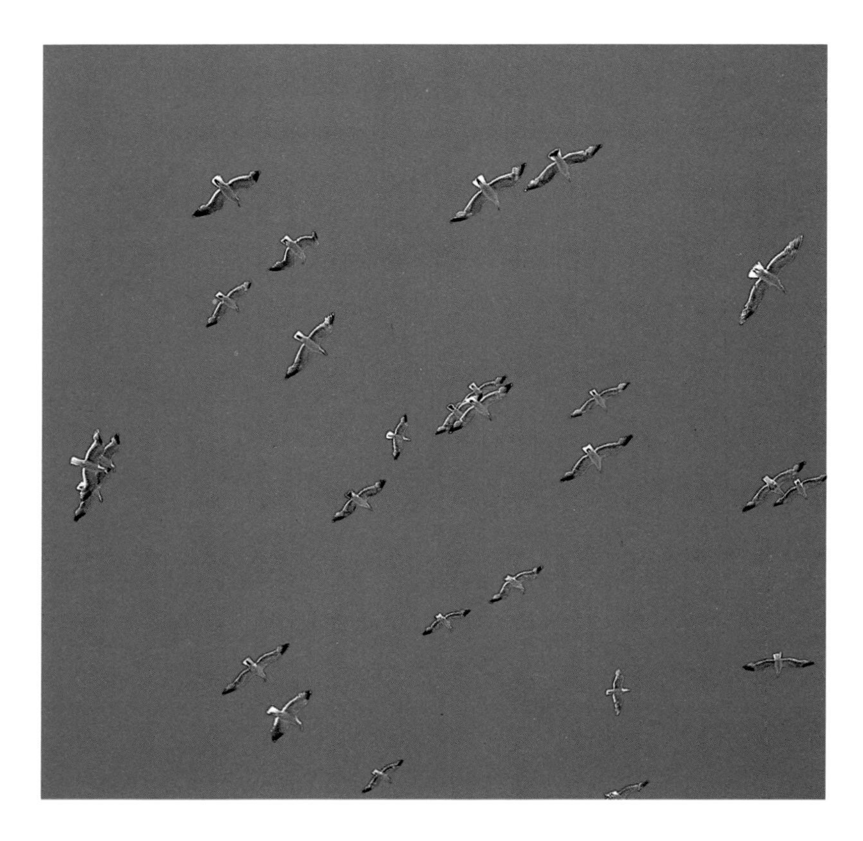

NO MATTER how rugged the conditions, life flourishes along the frontier between land and sea. The fluctuations in temperature, humidity, tides, climate and currents all serve to increase the varieties of life forms. Life thrives and is strengthened by adverse conditions; the active multiply and the indolent vanish.

Each member of this incredible community is dependent upon the other, and because these life forms are rather backward by man's rather self-satisfied standards, they do not need planning commissions, governmental agencies, courts, written rules or advice columnists to tell them how to conduct their lives.

Yet these relationships between eater and eaten are so complex yet so basic that man can barely comprehend the framework of these interdependencies. We see the parts but never the whole. We see the individual species from the gulls overhead to the clams a few inches beneath our feet. We photograph, paint and sculpt images of some and dig and eat others. Obviously we are part of this baffling food chain, but we continue to seek what we assume is a deeper understanding. When asked why, we respond with the pat answers about man's inate curiosity. Could it simply be that we are incurable meddlers?

The study of shore creatures continues to be infinitely rewarding. Many of us take these studies seriously and we earn our livings from the sea. Few occupations, either for income, pleasure or both, are more enjoyable than studying bird life along the shore.

The Pacific Coast is famous among birdwatchers for its so-called Pacific Flyway, the route taken by birds that migrate back and forth between the Arctic and tropics of Latin America. Birdwatchers have learned to predict the arrivals of various species each year and certain estuaries of rivers that yield food and resting areas are occupied during these migrations by both man and bird. Several refuges have been set aside for the migratory birds to insure their survival as a species.

One great shorebird viewing area is in Washington around the 94-square-mile Grays Harbor estuary. During one weekend biologists counted more than one million shorebirds that had stopped by for food and rest. The most abundant species here are Western Sandpiper, Dunlin, Short-billed and Long-billed Dowitchers and Red Knot. A few rare birds, such as the Peregrine Falcon, are also spotted from time to time. Biologists now believe these migrations have been occurring since the Pleistocene Age.

Other famous migrations include the swallows that return to San Juan Capistrano in California each year. In one of the greatest migrations of all, the monarch butterfly trek from Canada and Alaska to the Monterey Peninsula each year. These black-and-orange insects have wintered each year for centuries beyond counting. Each October they flock to Point Pino, up to three million of them, arriving singly, in small groups or by the thousands, swooping down low when they arrive at Monterey Bay, barely missing fishing and pleasure boats. They crowd into some three acres of Monterey pines, locally called the "butterfly pines." There they cling to the branches and bark throughout the winter. Sometimes they become chilled and fall to the ground harmlessly, and awaken from their stupor when the sun comes up and thaws them.

Their navigational apparatus remains largely a mystery, although there is evidence that they use polarized light as a guide as do bees and ants.

The nearby town of Pacific Grove has both capitalized on their winter residents and gone to great lengths to protect them. Festivals are held in their honor, and the local government has established a $500 fine plus a jail sentence for persons molesting these insects.

WHEN people with an artistic or aesthetic bent speak of the coast in those terms, many listeners quickly become restless, because words such as "artistic" and "aesthetic" and phrases such as "emotional impact" and "the balance of nature" sound pretentious. Yet they, too, are responding to all these needs that mere words cannot adequately express.

Man's need for the sea is expressed in more blunt economical terms: Land on the ocean shore costs more throughout the world than any other land, and it isn't simply because it is in more limited supply.

So we keep going back to the seashore, dipping our toes, swimming and sailing on the surface of the source of all life on earth. Those who sail along the coast, such as this group of ocean-class sailboats off Long Beach, California, usually stay near the shore, and many sail for the relaxation it offers; only you, the boat, the ocean, the wind and the sky for a few hours each week.

Those who go on extended sailing expeditions across the oceans can become as addicted to the sea as a victim of drugs, and all time spent on shore between voyages is time wasted in waiting for the next voyage. Most dedicated sailors will say they have destinations to reach, but these destinations are always followed by another and another, so that it is quickly clear that it is the journeys that matter, not destinations.

Scattered along the shoreline are many structures made by man which have their own beauty, just as those made by sea creatures have theirs. While we tend to be more critical of manmade structures on the grounds that they are not "natural," who is to say what is and what is not natural? If a barnacle builds himself a dwelling, why can't man? If a crab finds himself a vacant shell and wanders around the tidal zone with it, is it so different than man traveling the shoreline in his own vehicle?

We obviously have our own selfish definitions of how the shoreline should be used, and we transfer these interests into philosophy. Granted, those who want the shoreline protected from destruction must be applauded, but a balance must be constantly struck between those who detest footprints in the sand and those who would cover the sand with concrete or asphalt. The same forces that maintain this balance among human endeavors are reflected in the balance struck in the tide pools by the continual jockeying for dominance. Should one species totally dominate the tide pools, the tide pools would quickly cease to exist.

So we continue our battles over the future of the coastal strip. Those who occupy land we desire are our competitors. Thus, our jealousy and greed are the basis of many shoreline disputes and are frequently cloaked in either emotional or aesthetic arguments. It is all part of the natural order of things, this competition for space and the use of the shoreline. Man goes to court to settle these disputes. Tide-pool creatures are more direct and final in their disputes; one eats the other, putting a permanent end to the discussion.

It has always been a point of amusement to observers of disputes over how man should conduct himself with creatures of the land and sea to note that most people who are avid anti-hunting critics see no contradiction by being avid fishermen. Even when this contradiction is pointed out to those opposed to all forms of hunting, they usually shrug it aside, firm in their belief that cold-blooded creatures are "different." They seem to feel a natural affinity with warm-blooded creatures and risk their lives and their incomes going to sea to fight against those who kill whales and seals and other mammals of the sea.

Fish are just different, they seem to be saying. They see nothing cruel about fishing for pleasure instead of food, and insist that a fish doesn't feel the hook even though blood flows. Sports fishermen are fond of using barbless hooks so that they can catch a fish on extremely lightweight line so that the fight is longer and more likely to result in a fish breaking the line and swimming away with a hook permanently embedded in its jaw.

If fish had legs or soft brown eyes and looked as cuddly as a deer, they would have millions of defenders among *homo sapiens.* They seem to be doing reasonably well without our help or emotional involvement, however, and only a few species hover on the edge of extinction. Most of these are landlocked rather than ocean dwellers. An exception is the salmon which makes itself very vulnerable by its need to spawn in freshwater streams. In this case, as in all cases of fish, the fears by man that it will become extinct reflect our fear of losing a good source of food instead of losing something that is beautiful—and pretty and cuddly.

TRY to imagine this scene on the Tillamook River in Oregon without the abandoned piling repeating itself in the early-morning sun and mist. Would it be more beautiful or more natural without manmade structures in the photograph? It is a debate without end because all beauty ultimately is a personal matter. What if the piling were new and the platform that once stood on them were still intact, and people were living and working on the dock or in the building the piling once supported? Few viewers would feel the same emotional impact because we respond more easily to old things than new. Is it because older things appeal to our secret wishes for immortality? Is it because old things have had a chance to develop their own identity and place in the order of things? Such questions have no final, complete answers because each of us feels differently toward such matters.

ALTHOUGH all fishermen hope to bring home something for their efforts, after going out on a morning such as this one in Tillamook Bay, the beauty of the day is sufficient reason to leave the house at dawn and cruise along the shore. Although most sports fishermen choose not to discuss such matters, still it is the beauty of the shoreline and the estuaries that attracts them as much as the prospect of bringing home food. It is the nature of many sportsmen that they combine the work ethic with their recreation, and feel that a day spent admiring the scenery with nothing to show for it is a waste of time. Many are not bothered by going out and not catching fish; at least they tried.

PUGET SOUND has often been called a boater's paradise. The water and weather aren't as warm and balmy as along the California Coast, but it is the only place between Canada and Mexico that has sheltered water and a great variety of scenery for boaters. One of the most spectacular, and often thrilling, trips is through Deception Pass, which separates Whidbey Island from Fidalgo Island. The latter is barely an island and is separated from the mainland only by the long, shallow Swinomish Slough, which gives boaters an alternate route when they don't want to attempt Deception Pass. In this narrow passage the water rushes through at each tide change, creating whirlpools and backwashes that can overturn small boats.

Deception Pass State Park, which surrounds the pass, is the most popular state park in Washington, yet is so large that thousands of people can be using it without anyone feeling crowded.

ONE of the most pleasant ways to see Puget Sound is by small plane at a low elevation. Then the patterns, such as this made by a fishing boat putting out its net, can be appreciated much more than from sea level. Puget Sound supports the largest boat population of any place along the Pacific Coast, and includes everything from small cruise ships to the tiny outboard-powered "kicker" boats so popular with salmon fishermen. Because the waters are sheltered, small boats are safer here than in most salt water along the coast.

YAQUINA BAY at Newport, Oregon, is without question one of the most beautiful harbors along the coast. With the elegant Yaquina Bay Bridge as a backdrop and the large population of commercial fishing boats and pleasure craft in the harbor, hardly a day goes by that you can't see a scene worthy of a Winslow Homer painting. Newport is in the heart of Oregon's series of state parks and beautiful beaches, and a great deal of marine biological and geological research is conducted in the area. Yaquina Bay is one of the best harbors along the rugged coastline. It is also the home of one of the busiest Coast Guard stations in Oregon.

NO matter how long you live on the coast—even if you are born there and are seldom out of sight of the surf—you never hear people describe it as a boring place to live. Even sedentary people who never go surfing or sailing in Hawaii find themselves drawn to scenes as peaceful and ordinary as this view of the curving patterns of waves washing up on the sand. One of the nicest things about living in Hawaii is that although it is definitely tropical, it has mountains on all islands. The islands are simply mountains that climbed out of the sea. Residents have their choice of living at or near sea level or a few hundred feet higher where the weather is a bit cooler. It is possible to spend an afternoon on the beach with the temperature in the 80s or 90s, then drive a few minutes up into the mountains and have weather cool enough for a fire in the fireplace.

THE shape of the waves washing on the shore of Bandon Beach in southern Oregon is copied by the twisted seaweed left behind when the tide moved back out to sea. Bandon is one of the most beautiful areas of the coast. The area is one of the least used because it is some distance from the highways that lead from the heavily populated Willamette Valley to the coast. But visitors are almost invariably charmed by this unpretentious town and the coastline that has broad, sandy beaches and dramatic rocks offshore.

FOAM created by an offshore storm becomes a subtle dressing for the calm, flat surf at Cannon Beach, Oregon, one of the most beautiful stretches of beach on the coastline. The first white visitors to the area were members of the Lewis and Clark party who wintered at Fort Clatsop near present Astoria in 1805-06. The small group of explorers went over Tillamook Head and down to the small Indian village at Cannon Beach to try and purchase some blubber off a whale that washed ashore. Decades later the small settlement there was named for a cannon found washed ashore from a shipwreck.

PEOPLE are dwarfed by the surf that follows the curving contours of this beach in Hawaii. From the beach such designs are not apparent, but seen from a headland or a low-flying plane, they show us the shore in a totally different interpretation.

ALL along the Pacific coastline are bits and pieces of evidence that most of the shore was at one time under the sea. This scene at Bowling Ball Beach near Noyo, California, shows the strata of stone that run from the cliffs down into the sea. This easily eroded stone was once simply sand, but was compressed by the weight of the earth and sea into stone, then uplifted by some monumental force beneath the earth's surface, creating the shoreline and shallow bay. Similar formations are found at intervals along the coast; some are composed of lava, others of limestone. Such formations are not common in the Hawaiian Islands, where lava flows from an underwater volcano are solely responsible for the islands' existence.

SOMETIMES patterns seen in one aspect of nature have a way of copying another form. For example, this could be a feather or a cloud formation. Like gazing at billowing clouds or staring into wood fires, watching the shape of waves and sand can become almost anything your imagination wants. Many visitors to the shore return home and are almost embarrassed when asked what they did because it is easy to spend an entire afternoon doing nothing more productive or strenuous than lying on the beach and watching the clouds and the waves and the shore birds. Or you will find yourself bent over for hours looking through beach rocks in search of agates or almost any small stone that has an interesting shape or color.

ADDED to the basic shapes in the surf are the important color schemes. This small stretch of beach at Kaanapali on Maui is beautifully tinted by the colors of the sunset, proving that all beauty in sunsets is not in the sky alone. Nearly every evening in Hawaii you will see tourists lined up on the beach watching the sunset show as though they are members of some religious cult that worships the sun or evening. Sunsets in the tropics are quite sudden events, especially at sea. Dawn and dusk last only a few minutes compared with the quite long periods of sunset and dusk in the desert or Great Plains.

SOMETIMES it is the details of a scene rather than all the elements combined that make it beautiful. This combination of rocks, coral, sand, sea and light at Ke'e Beach on Kauai is an example. Kauai is the most remote of the inhabited Hawaiian Islands and is older than the others. The islands were formed by volcanoes in an area where the earth's plates keep moving slowly over the centuries. Apparently the islands began at Midway, then gradually built down the chain of reefs and islets that lead to the Hawaiian Islands. The other islands have slowly eroded away, and all the major islands now are being gradually scoured by the rain and wind. Many centuries from now the present islands will have worn away. Only the Big Island of Hawaii is still growing. Apparently still another island is being formed by volcanic action and lava flows southeast of the Big Island. Now it is only a seamount, but as the action continues, it will eventually rise above the surface of the ocean to become the newest of the chain.

NORMALLY fishing on the shore is a calm and sedate form of recreation, but there are exceptions, such as when the smelt come ashore at Yachats, Oregon, to lay their eggs on the coarse "pepper and salt" volcanic sand common there. Other similar events include the grunion runs on the beaches of southern California when they come up to the beach to spawn. Both species have intricate sets of signals embedded in their genes which send them ashore at just the right time. The grunion make their spawning runs during the high tides after each full and new moon between February and sometimes as late as August. Because the sport has become so popular, the season is closed during April and May to insure that propagation continues as the fish intend. In each case, the eggs of grunion and smelt must be laid and covered, and remain moist until they hatch.

Some people think these tiny fish are either suicidal or, like the salmon, that they come home to spawn and die. Not so. Both species come in riding high on the waves, squirm frantically to dig a slight depression on the beach into which the eggs can be deposited and fertilized. Then they swim back to sea and, if they survive another egg-laying and fertilization cycle, return again to the same spot to repeat the performance.

Some fish are equally at home in fresh and salt water, and for reasons nobody has quite uncovered, most of these fish insist on spawning in either fresh water or in shallow water where danger to themselves and their eggs is the highest. Here, fishermen with dip nets and buckets are scooping up the smelt that make an annual run to the beaches, where not only man but virtually every other creature of the tidal zone can easily pluck them from the water. Other smelt runs are made up from the tributaries of the Columbia River, particularly the Cowlitz River before the eruption of Mt. St. Helens in 1980 covered the beds with silt. The fish also go up the Lewis River, the Sandy River and some smaller tributaries, answering some instinct we may never understand.

Three main species of smelt live in the Northwest. The best known is the so-called Columbia River smelt, or the eulachon *(Thaleichthys pacificus)*. The second species, shown here, is the surf smelt *(Hypomesus Pretiosus)*. A third and much more scarce species is the long-finned smelt *(Spirinchus dilatus)*, which lives in Lake Washington and Harrison Lake in British Columbia.

The surf smelt is much smaller than the Columbia River species and, thus, less of a commercial fish. Yachats, Oregon, gets the most each year, followed by Grays Harbor and several places around Puget Sound and Hood Canal. The small town of La Conner, Washington, on the Swinomish Channel just off Puget Sound, has an annual smelt derby, whether the smelt come or not.

Some towns have held smelt-eating contests in conjunction with their arrival, with the one at Kelso, Washington, the best known such gastronomical event. The tiny, oily fish present a major challenge to contestants after the first two dozen are consumed.

Longtime observers of the Columbia River smelt runs believe the main body of the annual migration is preceded by a "scouting party" of only a few hundred that heads up the Columbia, then drifts back down to rejoin the main force before starting the real migration. Their progress can be followed by watching the seagulls gathering around the shallow-swimming smelt and gorging themselves on those who venture too near the surface.

MORE than any other activity on the beach, groups of people digging for clams symbolize enjoyment of the beaches and the relationship between man and parts of the food chain along the shore. True, beaches represent sunbathing, volleyball, solitary walks, surfing, sailing, sand castles and a host of other activities, but digging for clams is at once a form of recreation and a part of our food-gathering work.

With the beaches offering so much food, particularly from northern California on to Alaska, it is easy to understand why the North Coast Indians had the leisure time to develop intricate social systems and an art and mythology that was unrivaled among North American Indians. Because food was so easy to gather, they had the time necessary to let their imaginations wander at will.

There were the foods of the shore—clams, mussels, salmon migrating up the streams, seaweeds—and the berries and fruits of the shore. The thick forests provided them with clothing, building material for long houses, and the giant trees, particularly the cedar, could be turned into either boats or the massive totems that told as much about their culture as European cathedrals and public buildings.

We must assume that the shoreline has always meant the same things to mankind. Long before the first white man arrived, and long before the first Chinese or Japanese ship was blown off course and landed on the western shores of North America, the first Indians who migrated southward from the Bering Strait felt that same combination of awe and peacefulness the shore gives us.

We can assume that Indian children built their versions of sand castles on the beaches and that after the evening meal they gathered to sit on driftwood and watch the sun disappear in the west.

All along the coast, especially near the rivers and streams that empty into the ocean, archaeologists have found evidence of long-abandoned Indian settlements. A few artifacts have been found, but most discoveries are little more than mounds of clam and other kinds of shells. They also find old firepits and an occasional stone that was used as a weapon or tool.

One of the most important seaside Indian villages for archaeologists is the village at Cape Alava on the Olympic Coast of Washington. Here a series of villages existed, each destroyed by mudslides from the steep mountain that rises directly behind the village site. Some of the landslides covered the village so completely that it sealed entire dwellings almost as intact as a museum, and through these well preserved artifacts, archaeologists have been able to piece together much of the tribe's lifestyle. The village was inhabited by Makah Indians, who have since moved to the Neah Bay area a few miles north. The Makahs were expert seamen and were whalers. All around the area are traces of their existence. A beach just south of the village is still

cleared of stones so the Makahs could launch and beach their boats there. Beach hikers frequently find stones with grooves in them, indicating they were used as net weights or anchors.

Most of the artifacts from the village have been taken to the Makah tribal museum at Neah Bay, which is one of the best tribal museums in the country.

The village at Cape Alava was one of the few major coastal villages that was not at the mouth of a major stream. However, the area has sufficient protection from heavy seas due to a long shelf of stone that goes some distance out to sea and a group of offshore islands that offers protection from heavy storms. Because of the nature of their existence, dependent as they were on the sea for their food and clothing, the Makahs were the best seamen in what is now the American Northwest Coast, and rivals to the great travelers and marauders from the north, the Haidas and Tlingits.

The Columbia River Indians, mostly members of the Chinook nation, were more likely to live away from the coast several miles and frequently some distance away from the Columbia River itself on the smaller rivers and creeks that feed into the large river. As the tide of white men continued to rise, most of the Chinooks became traders with the white men, and the language they developed, a combination Indian and English languages, became universally known as Chinook jargon. It is still spoken to a small degree among some of the older Indians. At one time each trader in the Pacific Northwest had to know how to speak it.

WHILE engineers talk of harnessing the ocean's energy to create electrical power, with plans for installing turbines in estuaries for the tides to turn, those who use the surf as a playground have their own uses for the enormous and constant energy expended in the waves. Surfing as we know it was invented by the Hawaiians, who used boards so heavy that only the strongest among the men could wrestle them out to sea. Now even the proverbial 90-pound weakling on the beach can handle them with ease due to their lightweight plastic construction. The best surfing in the world is in the Hawaiian Islands, where this group of surfers is watching a wave curl in on Sunset Beach on Oahu.

THE Kona Coast of the Island of Hawaii isn't as good for surfing as those on Oahu and some other islands, and the beaches are fewer due to the recent volcanic eruptions that have covered beaches with lava. But dotted along the Kona Coast are small and beautiful pockets of sandy beach suitable for body surfing, as this group shows, on White Sand Beach. This island continues to grow in popularity with visitors who prefer as much variety as possible in scenery and climate. The Kona Coast tends toward a desert ecology and has many square miles of wasteland from relatively recent lava flows. The Hilo side has frequent rain, many overcast days and the lush vegetation we commonly associate with the tropics.

SOME Hawaiian beaches are better for looking than surfing, such as this stretch on Maui near the resort complex at Kaanapali Beach, where the foam creates a soft fringe along the beach. The Kaanapali Beach Resort complex, a group of highrise hotels and golf courses and shopping centers, is an example of how a stretch of land not usable for agriculture can be turned into a valuable asset. The major property owners in the Hawaiian Islands are sugar cane and pineapple companies, and their land on the western end of Maui was of no commercial value until the Kaanapali resort area was developed. Now it is one of the most popular resorts in the islands.

BODY surfing isn't for the faint of heart, but it gives a thrill when the great energy of the waves thrusts you along on the crest toward a sandy beach, such as this one at Poipu Beach in Kauai. This island is in many ways the most beautiful in the Hawaiian chain, yet one of the least developed. Because its coastline is so wild and untouched by roads and resort developments, it has been used as the setting for a number of motion pictures, such as *South Pacific, Hawaii, Sadie Thompson* and others. At the Coco Palms Resort stands a small church that was built for a set during the filming of *Sadie Thompson.* The resort management asked the film crew to leave it standing, and since then more than 1,000 weddings have been held there.

IN spite of the similarity of each breaker coming in to crash against the land, one seldom grows tired of watching their endless march across the Pacific. This enjoyment is heightened when a stiff offshore breeze clips the tops off them and creates a flurry of spindrift flying in the opposite direction. This windy day occurred at Beverly Beach on the Oregon Coast. One of the most difficult laws of physics related to the sea to comprehend is that the waves we see aren't really moving water; instead, they are created by energy moving through the water. As evidence of this, watch a piece of wood or other object near the shore on a windless day with a heavy surf. The object floating on the surface will naturally rise and fall with the waves, but it will hardly change its position as the waves continue crashing against the shore.

ONE of the best places for watching winter storms batter the coast is at Shore Acres State Park near Coos Bay, Oregon. Here the surf pounds directly against the cliffs, leaving behind a residue of spray and mist that drifts upward into the timber. On days with surf as heavy as this, you can feel the reverberations hitting the cliffs as you stand on the overlook, and you should be prepared for a soaking for both you and your car. This state park has much more to offer than views of the surf. It was once the home of a shipping magnate named Lewis J. Simpson, who built a mansion and imported plants from all over the world. The property eventually was deeded to the State of Oregon, but the mansion was razed. Only a part of the building remains. The oriental gardens and most of the original landscaping are still intact making it one of the more unusual parks along the coast.

ONE of the greatest scenes on the coast is watching the breakers come rushing in after a storm, crashing and exploding with dull, jarring sounds. Often the waves will climb far above the cliffs, as these are at Shore Acres State Park in Oregon. The energy carried by waves is almost beyond comprehension. Many years ago when the lighthouse on Tillamook Rock near Seaside, Oregon, was manned, during a particularly bad storm the sea picked up a rock weighing 135 pounds and hurled it more than 100 feet high. It hit the roof of the lighthouse and fell through, causing a great deal of damage.

BECAUSE the Hawaiian Islands have no equivalent of the Continental Shelf to change the configuration of the waves before they reach the shoreline, the waves strike the islands with more force than the mainland. During periods of extremely heavy seas, scenes such as this on the Na Pali Coast of Kauai are common. The islands are particularly vulnerable to giant waves created by underwater earthquakes called either seismic waves or tsunamis.

BREAKERS have an endless variety of patterns, depending on which stretch of coast they strike. This rocky shoreline along the Oregon Coast creates a series of hurdles for the waves to crash over, each stage of the rocks creating different patterns. Occasionally we read about a rogue wave or the so-called seventh wave crashing up on the shore with considerably more force than any of the others, creating some damage. Such waves definitely do exist, although scientists aren't quite certain why or how they are created.

ALTHOUGH all heavy waves coming in have their awesome appearance and they appear different depending on the amount and quality of light striking them, they often can be stunningly colorful. The sunlight striking this wave along the California Coast gives it a translucent green virtually no combination of paint could duplicate. Actually, many artists who are adept at painting skies and clouds and other parts of nature are often baffled and defeated when attempting to paint accurate marine scenes because there are so many different textures and subtleties of color in the ocean.

WHILE some of the most spectacular breaker explosions occur when they hit cliffs and headlands, the dull explosions and brilliant spray caused by two waves colliding is equally impressive. This frequently occurs where the ocean bottom and prevailing tidal currents cause waves to turn at an angle to the land and collide with the waves coming directly in toward land. These are the kinds of seas dreaded by Coast Guardsmen because too many small boaters and fishermen decide it is safe to leave harbors, only to capsize in the surf. Some of the Coast Guard's most exciting—and too often disastrous—rescues are made under these conditions.

THE SEA is constantly moving, restlessly flowing in great circles around the Pacific, a series of vast rivers composed of the same waters that are subject to the spinning of the earth, the tidal pull of the moon and, to a much lesser extent, the wind. Each ocean and each of the smaller divisions called seas have their own currents that sweep back and forth across the open ocean and up and down the coastlines. The most famous, of course, is the Gulf Stream that sweeps northward through the Caribbean Sea.

Yet these great saline rivers have little or no effect on the breakers that pound against the shoreline. These great waves created by storms and strong winds are only a surface disturbance while the rest of the ocean, from seldom deeper than two hundred feet on down to the floor, ignores these local disturbances. The energy that creates these waves moves horizontally rather than vertically. A creature of the deepest part of the ocean is no more aware of these heavy surfs than we are of shifts in the jet stream thousands of feet over our heads.

YET we are profoundly affected by these ocean currents, just as we are the changing patterns in the jet stream, because the ocean currents create our climate to a large extent. The so-called Japanese Current that sweeps from the tropics north past Japan and around the Aleutian Islands before swinging back southward again against Canada and America's West Coast is what brings much of the Pacific Northwest's temperate but wet weather. If that current picked up more water from the Arctic before swinging southward, our climate along the West Coast would be several degrees colder. And that same current creates different water temperatures at the same latitude. When it passes Japan after leaving the tropics it is several degrees warmer off those islands than, it is at the same latitude on the American side of the ocean. This climate control by the ocean results in a very consistent climate along the shoreline, and reaches its peak of control in the Monterey and Carmel area where the temperature varies no more than 10 degrees throughout the year.

MANY mornings following storms are clear and sunny, giving visitors to the coast great shows as the waves continue to crash against the shoreline. For years many resort areas on the Pacific Coast were convinced that only fair weather and calm seas would be of interest to tourists, and were shocked at suggestions to advertise anything other than Miami Beach weather and scenery when no hurricanes were in sight. But over a period of years the resorts came around to advertising what the Pacific Coast had to offer—the stunning scenery with a touch of wildness to it, plus the great storms that sweep in from the ocean and provide excitement instead of only postcard palm trees and sand. Now some areas advertise the winter storms, and resort owners expect many guests from the inland cities to drive over for a weekend of storm watching and beachcombing after the storm blows away. The parking lots will be filled with people during these periods, particularly in Oregon where the coastline lends itself to wave watching. Much of the Washington Coast is away from the highway, although along the Long Beach Peninsula are a few places where you can sit in your car and watch the show. Occasional stretches of highway below the Olympic National Park coastal strip are also accessible. California, too, has storms, particularly in the north, but few big ones strike southern California.

All the Hawaiian Islands have their excellent storm-watching areas that offer an alternative to lying on calm beaches.

While the sea is constantly grinding away at the shoreline and wearing it down one grain of sand at a time, during these storms you can frequently hear the waves pounding a boulder against another or against the bluffs. While most of this erosion is almost invisible to us, sometimes after a severe storm the first person to walk out onto a headland will see that a section of a cliff or a boulder is missing. Sometimes entire headlands are undercut and fall into the ocean. Homes and entire villages have been lost in this manner.

The Northwest Coast is littered with millions of board feet of timber and stumps that break loose from their moorings in rivers, drift out to sea and then are pushed back to shore by the wind and currents. Virtually every beach from Cape Flattery to Crescent City, California, and further south have logs piled on them. It is much too costly to remove them and sell them for lumber, so they remain on the beaches, a great source of firewood for residents with four-wheel drive vehicles and chainsaws, and convenient picnic tables for beach hikers.

During a storm, however, these logs can be extremely dangerous, and hardly a year passes without a news report of someone being killed or badly injured while walking on logs that are struck by a wave and flung around.

Not all beachcombing is so potentially dangerous. After storms is the best time to go out and see what has been lost or abandoned by other people. The most popular item, of course, are those glass floats used for centuries by Japanese fishermen. Judging from the thousands if not millions that have been found from Alaska to Mexico, the Japanese must have had a major industry of manufacturing the floats. They are becoming fewer and fewer, however, because most fishnet floats now are made of cheaper and less attractive plastic. But the search continues all along the West Coast with every beachcomber hoping to find that prize, a perfect glass float.

Sometimes this search for the bounty of the sea takes on an almost slapstick situation. One winter a barge loaded with finished lumber began taking on water and finally was flipped over not far off the mouth of the Columbia River. Within a few hours two-by-fours and other lumber began washing up on the beach. Trucks, pickups, Jeeps, sedans and various other kinds of vehicles began arriving to haul away the prize. The beach soon began looking like a giant playground as the impromptu salvage crew jockeyed for position and loaded the lumber as quickly as possible. A few fistfights broke out when two men grabbed the same piece of lumber at the same time.

During World War II the beachcombing wasn't nearly so pleasant and profitable, particularly during the early months of the war when Japanese submarines visited the West Coast and sank a few vessels. Although the toll was much higher on the East Coast where German submarines sank many, many vessels, still those along the West Coast were never certain when they might go for a walk on the beach only to find some grisly memento of the war.

ONCE you have been to the shore, you find yourself going back again and again to the same places, knowing they will be the same, yet never identical. The effects of erosion may not be immediately obvious on the beach and offshore rocks and the headlands, but the intricate combination of weather and tides is never quite the same from day to day, season to season. The cloud formations are certainly never identical, and even overcast days with a flat gray sky and flat gray sea beneath are never identical.

The earth may have stretches of landscape that we consider lacking in beauty to the point of ugliness. Some people cannot bear the flat, open scenery of deserts and plains, but those same people will look at a flat, calm sea and feel they have been treated to a visual delight. One almost never hears the sea and shore described in disparaging terms. True, some sections are more beautiful than others, but we find it virtually impossible to think of anything connected with the coastline as unattractive.

Why this is true is a question for philosophers, poets and psychologists to answer. Part of it may be our fascination with large things—the higher mountains, the biggest river, the largest lakes, not to mention airplanes, automobiles and other manmade structures. But the sea is so large that it is almost beyond comprehension. To speak of its measurements is to enter the realm of distances measured in light years, ages in terms of billions of years and power measured in megatons. We can easily mouth the words but we do not always comprehend what we said. Nor can we really comprehend the forces that created the earth, no matter whether we accept the Big Bang theory, the version given in Genesis or that of other religions throughout the world. All of them are so far beyond anything that man has experienced in recorded history that none of us could write a scenario to approach the magnitude of the events involved in creation.

We can only suppose that when the earth was a molten ball of matter, a part of a sun that exploded and created our solar system—that before the cooling process was completed, there was one more event that resulted in the creation of the moon. The version given by many scientists is that the moon was a piece of the earth that spun off with a force that would make our atomic and hydrogen and proton bombs firecrackers by comparison.

The moon, however it came into being, is the strongest single force exerted on the ocean with the twice-daily tidal cycles that are felt in all bodies of water of any magnitude. It is this tidal pull that stops and reverses the flow of the mighty Columbia River, and its effect is felt as far upriver as Bonneville Dam more than 100 miles from the Columbia River bar.

One version of earth's creation is that when the earth was still composed of liquids that had not congealed into

land and water, the sun exerted such a tremendous tidal pull that the liquids swirled and sloshed around the earth, barely held together by the earth's gravity while the planet slowly hardened into rock. Because the earth spun on its axis and the sun kept up its steady pull, the tidal waves grew and grew until the force of their oscillation and that of the earth was too much. A large wave, larger than we can possibly imagine, was torn off with other matter and whirled off into space to become the moon.

Whatever forces and events were behind the creation of the earth, we know only that the moon and the seas remain, and that many creatures of the sea have evolved around this constant tidal pull. Much of the shape of the coastline is related to this constant flooding and ebbing of the tides.

Some stretches of coastline are particularly vulnerable to the tides, and due to the configuration of these inlets, the tides rush in and out with the force of a major river. The most extreme examples of this are the Bay of Fundy on the East Coast and Cook Inlet in Alaska. The tidal range varies from place to place depending on a variety of factors, including the size of the body of water, the configuration of the ocean floor and the shoreline itself. For example, on the Atlantic side of the Panama Canal, the range is little more than one or two feet; on the Pacific it has a range of 12 to 16 feet. The range is usually quite low, seldom more than two feet, on Pacific islands, and the range is slight in California compared with parts of Oregon and most of Washington.

WHILE we think of seascapes as being vacant of man-made structures, sometimes the more elegant designs of man add a new dimension to scenes, such as this showing the Deception Pass Bridge against a late-afternoon sky in Washington's Puget Sound. Seen from this vantage point, the bridge shows the same attention to detail and structure as a spider web and is no more out of place in the scheme of things than a web.

This bridge is a favorite gathering spot for visitors to the north end of Whidbey Island. During beautiful weather it will be lined with people watching the small boats fight their way through the series of whirlpools and riptides that occur when the tide is moving either in or out through the narrow passage. The bridge is divided into two spans connected at a tiny island in the center of the passage, where you can walk down trails almost to the water's edge and watch the currents whip back and forth.

THE morning scenery along the West Coast tends to be more gentle, more subtle and with a blending of soft colors; not the primary colors of sunsets. Here a soft veil of autumn fog rises along the Oregon Coast at Cape Meares State Park with the tinted sunrise slanting across it.

Although the Oregon Coast is host to more visitors in the summer months than any other time of the year, many visitors prefer waiting for the crowds to leave before going to the coast in early autumn. Frequently some of the best weather conditions are found in the autumn months with clear, still and sunny weather and slightly chilly nights.

NO matter how much seamen have yearned for land, all through the centuries they have dreaded those last few miles; that is where most of the groundings and sinkings occur. The history of maritime activity along the West Coast is filled with records of ships that came too close to the shore and lost their maneuverability or were the victims of poor navigation or a host of other difficulties. Markers that are little more than gravestones with stories written on them are dotted along the coastline. One is the Norwegian Memorial, erected after the three-masted bark *Prince Arthur of Norway* went aground on the Olympic Peninsula of Washington, claiming 18 lives. Some 70 years later a touching memorial was held when the son of the skipper made a journey to America to see where his father had died. Remnants of other shipwrecks are found all along the Pacific Coast, grim reminders that it isn't always the sea alone that brings grief and death to seamen; it is often where land and sea meet that the worst problems occur.

EVENTUALLY all writers discussing the shoreline must yield to descriptive phrases as "clinging stubbornly" and "precarious toeholds" to describe the plant life that lives and thrives along the shoreline. This is especially true of the trees that sprout and live on exposed rocks such as this one in California. Over the years the wind and salt spray bend these trees inland with most branches able to grow only on the inland side away from the wind and spray. Thus they take on a combed look, as if they were daily flattened downward by the wind, like a mother determined to defeat a cowlick on a son's head.

THE Long Beach Peninsula, a broad and flat stretch of land separating the sea from Willapa Bay just north of the Columbia River, is one of the longest such strands in the world. The beach runs without interruption by rocks and headlands more than 30 miles due north from North Head and Cape Disappointment. A varied community of small towns has grown up along both sides of this peninsula, with oysters, commercial fishing, resorts, nurseries and cranberry farms as part of the local economy. Since the Columbia Bar is nearby, which has the reputation of being the roughest stretch of coast anywhere in America, the Coast Guard has a very busy station there that has participated in some of the most dramatic rescues in history. And because of this rough water, the Coast Guard long ago established a training school for its boat coxswains so they can have the benefit of the worst possible water for training and the best possible teachers, who are veterans of rescues at the mouth of the Columbia.

ALTHOUGH our eyes are constantly drawn to the grand scenes of the apparently endless sea and sky, it is often the smaller details that give perspective to the shoreline, such as the way waves curl around a small lava rock along the coast. One can become almost mesmerized by watching such activities along the shore and noting how it changes from minute to minute, tide to tide. Each time such a rock is uncovered by a low tide, walking out to it invariably gives a sense of discovery. When a group of rocks are slowly uncovered by the receding tide, it is almost like watching a time-lapse film that shows flowers blooming. And even though we know nothing different will be on the beach since the last low tide, still the initial urge is to follow the tide out and see what the sea has uncovered.

THE most remote stretch of coastline along the Washington Coast is contained within the ocean strip of the Olympic National Park, and one of the most spectacular stretches of scenery is Point of Arches, which can be reached only by hiking several miles along good trails. This is one of the roughest stretches of coastline in America with frequent heavy storms crashing in. Rainfall is measured in hundreds of inches. This constant erosion has worn down the former lava headlands and created these offshore seastacks and carved tunnels through several of the rocks. Not far away is a relatively recent shipwreck that can be reached at low tide by walking through one of these tunnels.

SOMETIMES one can hike a few hundred feet away from the shoreline into the thick forest and see another kind of beauty that, while related to the sea, is more of the forest. While the air may be laden with the smell of the sea, and the surf may be muffled and sound like a distant wind in the forest, still one has the sensation of being in a primeval forest before the arrival of man on the planet.

LOW tide in the Cape Flattery area of Washington is one of those special times when hikers can quickly lose themselves in the mysteries of the tide pools. Many tidepool areas along the coast near resort areas or highway approaches have been virtually stripped of life by visitors who either know no better or think that just one more starfish or just one more mussel or sea urchin won't be missed. Visitors should be aware of the damage they can do simply by walking on barnacle- and mussel-encrusted rocks, and children should be taught when young to look but don't touch while exploring in the tide pools.

SOME artists and photographers have devoted major portions of their careers to portraying patterns along the shore, such as this skeleton of an ancient Monterey Cypress in Point Lobos State Reserve. This part of the coastline has been immortalized in the muscular poetry of Robinson Jeffers, who wrote some of the most memorable American poetry in a stone tower he built overlooking the coast. The Monterey Coast and Big Sur just a few miles south have a reputation of attracting creative people. It began in the depression years of the 1930s when it was easy to find abandoned shacks left over from the time when state prisoners were used for laborers to construct Highway I, which follows the California Coast most of its length. Writers, artists, poets and assorted riff-raff found the natural beauty, the remoteness and the benevolent climate to their liking and established a tradition there that has lingered on for more than four decades.

LUPINE is one of the most common flowers along the West Coast. A member of the pea family, lupine appears in a wide variety of colors—blue or purple, white, and yellow. The bushy yellow variety seen all along the coast was a native of California that was introduced to Oregon and Washington to help control sand dunes.

SKUNK cabbage is one of the first flowers to bloom in the spring, and small glades near the coast will almost suddenly burst forth with the rich yellow blossoms. The plant carries a pungent odor that is reminiscent of skunk spray, but it isn't as offensive or as strong. This odor is released by the plant to attract carrion beetles, flies and other insects so they can spread the plant's pollen.

WILD azaleas grow profusely along the California and southern Oregon Coasts, and both states have set aside areas to help perpetuate their growth. Masses of them grow in the Brookings, Oregon, area. Others are scattered in the forests along the northern California Coast, and as far north as the Florence area of Oregon.

THE state flower of California, the California Poppy, is one of the most prolific and beautiful flowers found along the West Coast. Although it is native to a wide area from southern Oregon through California, it is a hardy plant that people can't resist taking home with them for their yards. Thus, its range is constantly spreading. A perennial plant, it grows from a hardy taproot, and its petals close at night and on dark days.

One of the most interesting of the coastal plants is the California pitcher-plant, or cobra-plant *(Darlingtonia californica)* which is found in bogs in northern California, the Siskiyou Mountains and along the Oregon Coast at various locations. The farthest north they are found is in the Florence, Oregon, area where the state has set aside a protected area for them to flourish. This is the only member of the pitcher-plant family in the West. They are constructed so that they serve their purpose of attracting and catching insects with ease. They are built like a tube that gradually widens from the base upward. Their crest is in the shape of a hood with a tip hanging downward that looks something like a fish tail. Nectar glands are on this fish-tail tip and inside the cavity. The interior is coated with downward-pointed hairs so that insects are directed on down toward the bottom of the tube. A fluid is secreted into the trap at the bottom; trapped insects drown in it and are digested by bacteria. Some of the digested material is absorbed into the plant's system to nurture it.

Undoubtedly some student of natural history has undertaken the job of identifying and totaling the number of plants that grow along the coastal strip of the West Coast. That total must run into the thousands, because it ranges from the mosses and lichen on rocks and trees to the giants of them all, the Redwoods.

Generally speaking, the coasts we speak of in this book, from Cape Flattery to southern California and the Hawaiian Islands, are in a moderate temperature zone. Although Cape Flattery is on the same latitude as Maine, that great ocean river of warmer water, the Japanese Current, keeps the offshore water warmer than its latitude would indicate. This current sweeps northward past the Japanese islands, then swings eastward past the Aleutian Islands (noted for their ferocious weather but not frigid temperatures), then down the West Coast of America.

The second factor in the mild weather of the Northwest Coast is the barrier against Arctic weather thrown up by the Cascade Range. This relatively low range is sufficiently high to block most of the Arctic storms that sweep down from Canada. The Cascades block most of the rainfall that comes in from the sea. Thus, you will find rainfall of more than 200 inches on the Olympic Peninsula and less than 200 miles away the desert or at least semi-desert ecology of eastern Washington and Oregon.

This moisture-laden air coming in off the Japanese Current is responsible for the frequent and heavy fog that cloaks much of the West Coast. Often the fog lies low to the ground, particularly in the low coastal hills of California, and an elevation of only a few hundred feet will be sufficient to be above this fog. In parts of the California Coast, residents have a choice of living directly on the coast and a short distance inland with the fog as a constant companion, or living slightly higher and having much more sun.

But it is this fog that nurtures the plant life along the coast, and without it much of the coastline would be given over to desert plants.

Flowers that grow along the coast have one of the longest blooming seasons of any flowers in America, generally from April to October. Depending on local conditions, some may bloom longer, others shorter. But it is a pleasant, mild life for plants that range from the rain forest of the Olympic Peninsula to the desert plants of southern California.

JUST as the birds and whales migrate up and down the coast, so do the seasons. It is possible to follow spring and summer up the coast early in the year, then reverse the voyage after summer ends. One of the most pleasant parts of a visit to the coast is taking the time to stop and examine the plant life that has adapted itself to the conditions along the coast. Since the climate ranges from hot to moderate—severe cold is rare anywhere from Baja California to the Strait of Juan de Fuca—the variety of wildflowers is astonishing, and each family of wildflowers has several divisions. Some species are found the entire length of the coastline, but the smaller and more delicate plants have gradually adapted themselves to the climatic conditions that range from the desert ecology to the lush rain forest conditions of the Pacific Northwest.

Both amateur and professional naturalists are fond of traveling the coast with identification books, and they often become as dedictated to searching for rare plants as birdwatchers. Unless a plant or flower grows profusely, it is best to leave flowers for others to see. Like creatures of the tide pools; it is easy to strip an area bare of flowers as each person thinks a single plucked flower won't affect the growth.

One flower that thrives along the coast and represents the delicate beauty found tucked away in little glades near the shoreline is the pink fawn lily, sometimes called the pink lamb's tongue. Its range is restricted almost entirely to the western coastline within a few steps of the beach on forest floors in shady areas.

One of the most beautiful types of wood that grows along the coast is the Oregon myrtle or California laurel *(Umbellularia californica)*. This is the well known myrtlewood that is found in shops along the coast, particularly in Oregon. Shops sell bowls, candlesticks, platters and a variety of other products made from this dark, beautifully grained wood. Unfortunately, some dealers stretch the truth a bit in advertising the wood. They make the claim that it grows only in the Holy Land and along the southern Oregon Coast. That isn't quite true. The myrtlewood of the Middle East is not the same as this species of laurel, although they are related. This species actually grows from around the Coos Bay area of Oregon to southern California.

One of the most interesting plant communities along the coast is the Pygmy Forest National Landmark near Caspar, California, between Mendocino and Noyo. Although several small areas of similar pygmy trees exist along the coast, this 600-odd acre preserve is the best example.

These plants are stunted by growing in a hardpan acidic soil that at the same time lets them survive without letting them grow naturally. Here visitors can see some of the tallest redwoods in existence and virtually at their base a pygmy redwood no taller than a man.

Some plants seem to thrive best on adversity, and the more difficulty they have surviving, the healthier and stronger they become over the years. An example is the cypress so common in the Monterey Peninsula area out of Point Lobos and Cypress Point. In fact, this species was once quite widely distributed along the coast but now grows in its natural state only in this area. The cypress trees have been photographed and painted so often that they are almost a symbol of the area with their contorted and mishapen trunks. They can be transplanted to other areas, and often are, but they do not thrive anywhere as well as they do in their native habitat where they are battered by the wind and the sea. They seem to grow quickly in more pleasant surroundings and make good windbreaks because of their fast and full growth. But apparently they "burn out" and die much younger than along the rocky coastline. It is something like putting a laborer behind a desk; the muscles turn to flab, and good health and life expectancy drop.

SOMETIMES the ocean makes headway in its continual pounding against the shore. This grove of giant spruce trees was gradually undermined by the ocean until they at last died. The shoreline near Cape Meares is lined with these dead giants. Frequently, such changes in the shoreline come when man makes changes in it, builds a jetty or dredges a bay. In the case of these dead spruce trees, it was a jetty built out from Tillamook Bay that changed the course of prevailing currents in the area. The beach was scoured away until the roots were inundated by saltwater or the trees were totally undercut by the sea and toppled over.

JUST as the pines and cypress trees are a signature on the California Coast, the madrona (or madrone) trees are common along much of the Pacific Coast. Madronas are particularly abundant in the sheltered inlets of Puget Sound. Although it is one of the most beautiful of the shore trees, it is also one of the messiest. It sheds its bark all during the summer months, which is shown here for its beauty rather than the untidy clutter found beneath all trees. And in the spring its leaves begin to fall, giving it roughly six months of shedding something onto the ground.

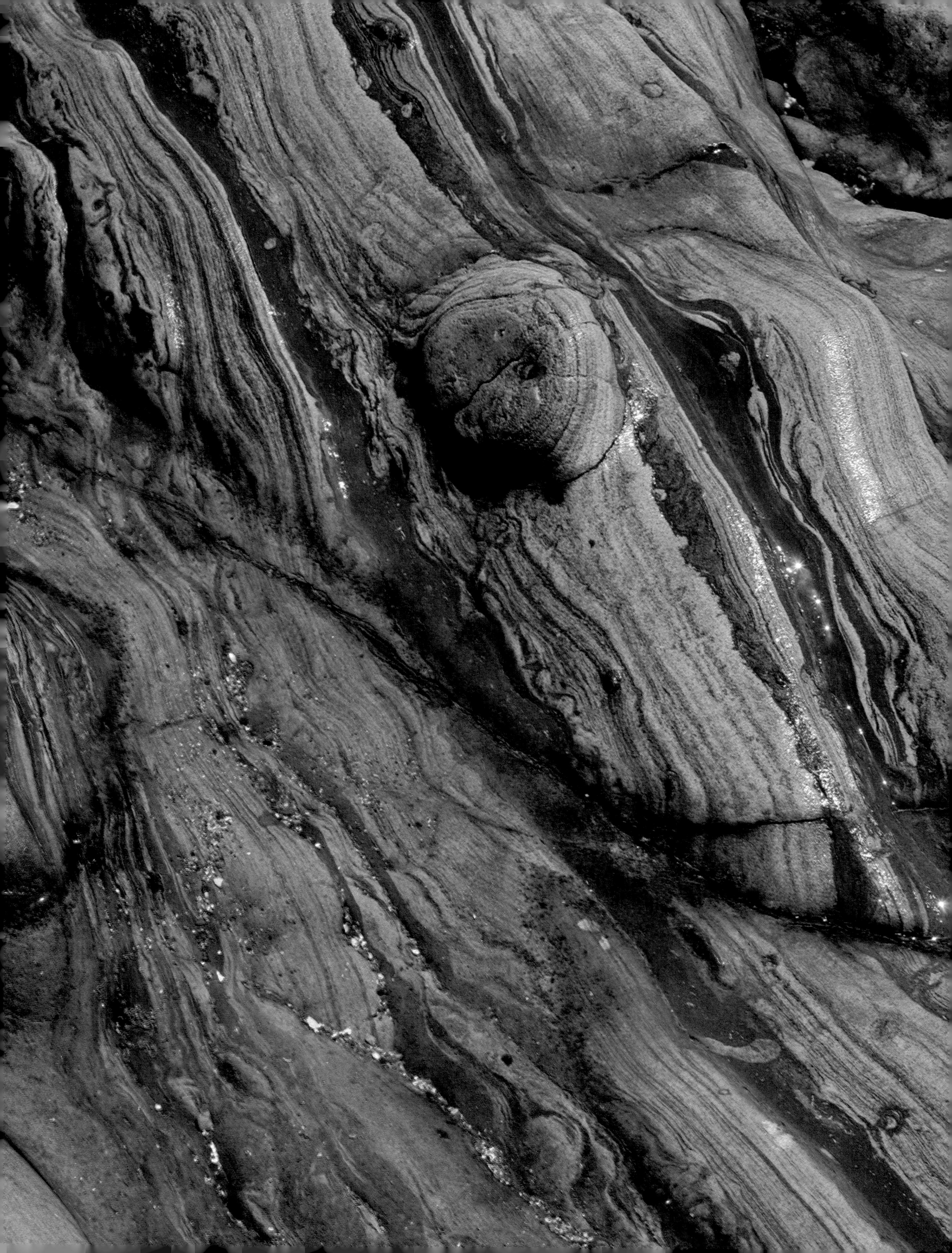

OTHER patterns are found in rock formations along the coast. The constant ebb and flow of tides and pounding by storms wear these colorful rocks on the California Coast to a smooth texture that is pleasing to see and touch. Naturalists, both professional and amateur, who specialize in the shore are usually mildly frustrated people because there is never enough time in one lifetime to explore all parts of the shore fully. Nearly all disciplines of natural science have their place on the coast, from archaeology to zoology.

A stroll along sections of coastline, such as this one in California, is a beautiful lecture in geology for those who understand something of the earth's crust and the various forces that caused it to rise from the sea eons ago. The colors and textures of these rocks change with the amount of light and water. Specialists in the earth sciences can tell us why such formations exist, but ask a child and you will be told much more fascinating stories of beasts and monsters and giants who created these images for us to ponder over.

OCCASIONALLY, the stones have a pattern and composition that make them look as though a sculptor created them and left them there for visitors' enjoyment. This unusual piece of sandstone sculpture lies on the shore of Point Lobos State Reserve in California. It could as easily be exhibited at a museum. Wherever rocks are found along the shore, similar sculptural images will be found. In areas where softer rocks such as sandstone are found, all sorts of shapes will occur. Small pieces of sandstone frequently are worn down by the sea until a small depression is formed. A tiny piece of harder rock that becomes trapped in the depression will eventually wear down the softer rock until a hole is worn completely through. How long this pestle effect takes to occur is beyond the patience of most people. It would take a carefully used grinding tool to achieve the same effect.

SOMETIMES beach visitors spend so much time looking down at the sand and rocks that they seldom see the entire grand scene. This attention to detail results in photographs such as this showing a small stream flowing down from nearby sandstone cliffs, creating a varied pattern and rich colors that change according to the time of day and the amount of sunlight filtering through the clouds and overcast. The scene will completely disappear when the tide moves in hard against the bluffs from which the stream flows.

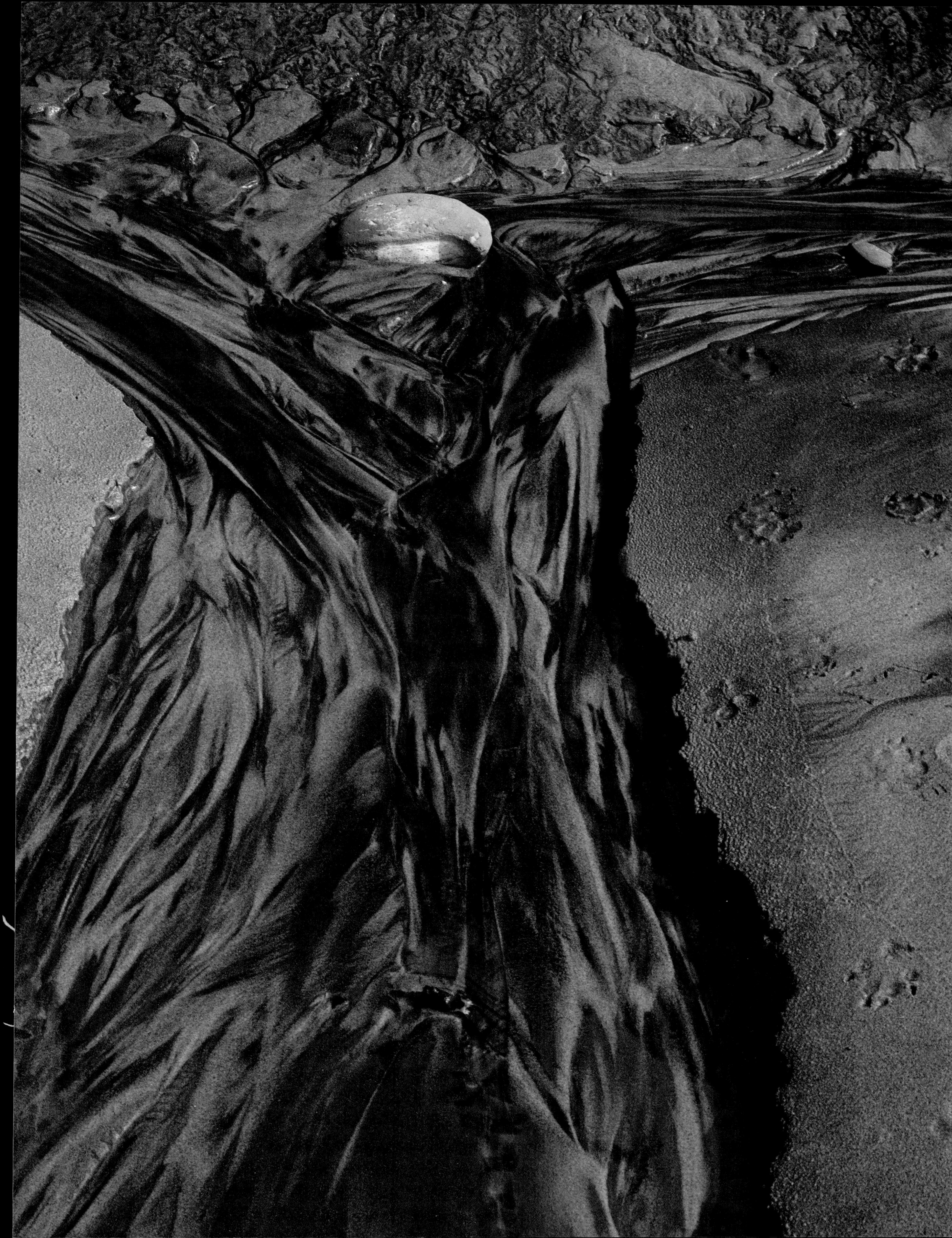

IN cool, clinical tones a geologist can tell you that these sandstone cliffs of Cape Kiwanda were created by the beach sand becoming compressed into soft stone, then uplifted from the shore through some violent movement in the earth's surface. All this is probably true, but you seldom think of such scientific matters when you're standing at the edge of one of the sandstone shelves watching the surf come in during the late afternoon when the red and dying sun paints everything in somber colors.

SCATTERED along the coastline of America are occasional "blow holes," resulting from lava tubes which permit the surf to wash in and out of them. Eventually a hole is eroded in the crust of the lava tube, letting the surf and the air virtually explode out of the holes, something like a whale spouting. This one is named Spouting Horn and is on the Poipu Coast of Kauai. Others can be found along the West Coast of the mainland from Baja California to Washington.

WHEN conditions are just right after a storm, foam that is churned by the waves and crashing surf will be blown up on shore to lie on the beach in depths of a few inches to two or three feet. This foam stays on the beach until all of the billions of bubbles finally bursts. This vast blanket of sea foam was washed up on Fogarty Creek State Park on the central Oregon Coast. This phenomenon does not occur after all storms, and those who are on the coast when the foam covers the beach count themselves fortunate in seeing this strange, harmless sight.

AFTER an afternoon shower, the sandstone cliffs of Cape Kiwanda in Oregon gleam in the last light of the day. This cape is a favorite with photographers and artists. Some have been known to camp near the cape for weeks on end so it can be recorded in all its moods, in all kinds of weather. Other than the pines at Point Lobos in California and Haystack Rock at Cannon Beach in Oregon, few landmarks have been photographed more on the coast. And those photographers and artists who have been there repeatedly insist on returning again and again in hopes of catching the cape in still another kind of light or with the sea in a new mood. There aren't many man-made objects that hold such a strong attraction.

AMONG the most awesome plants of the world, the redwoods of California have been a battleground between those who want to save some and those who want to cut them. This grove, cloaked in a veil of gentle fog, is along the northern California Coast. Only a few have been found growing naturally across the border in Oregon. Because these redwoods grow so well in areas of frequent fog, they're sometimes called the "poets of fog." The fog is obviously important if not vital to their existence. It protects them from the hard, drying rays of the sun, and this fog belt has in a sense defined the limits of the coast redwood. This variety *(Sequoia sempervirens)* is the tallest tree in the world and grows within an area roughly 450 miles long by no more than 30 miles wide mainly in California. It is related to the "giant Sequoia" of the Sierra Nevada range but they have major differences. The coast redwood has great commercial value for housing and furniture construction. The inland relative has very little value because its wood is given to shattering.

ALL along the Northwest Coast small, unnamed streams trickle down from the wet Olympic Mountains, cross the beaches and return to the sea. Many of these streams have a rusty color due to all the dead vegetation they flow over and through. Hikers along the coast must boil or chemically treat the water before drinking it. Still, in spite of the heavy rainfall along the Olympic Coast, hikers can go for several miles between streams. During the peak of summer, many creeks dry up completely, making one wonder just where all that rainfall goes after it hits the western face of the Olympic Mountains.

ALTHOUGH each of us would like to own property overlooking scenes such as this at Samuel H. Boardman State Park in Oregon, we are also pleased that the State of Oregon took control of nearly all of the coastline and made it available to all people, not just a fortunate few. The Oregon Coast is unique in the country for this public ownership of so much prime real estate. Consequently much of this coastline has retained its original appearance, and few structures intrude on the scenery. Samuel Boardman is often referred to as the father or creator of Oregon state parks as they now exist.

IF the coastline consisted only of long, sweeping beaches of sand without rocks, tide pools or coral reefs, many people would never see the fascinating and beautiful forms of life that live at the edge of land and sea.

This sunflower starfish is one of the most rare of the widespread and varied species. It has up to 24 arms and consequently is the fastest-moving member of the starfish family.

Starfish are one of the most common of the carnivores on rocks along the tidal zone. They wander about over the rocks at their own slow pace and attack mussels, snails, sea urchins and other members of the community. This attack is not a leaping or sneaking approach. Rather, the starfish simply move over the target creature, then wrap themselves aroung the creature and squeeze until the shell is crushed or those meals without shells are reduced to an easily managed mass of flesh.

In the case of creatures with shells, the starfish often has to pry them open, holding one edge of the shell with its foot and pulling mightily with its arms. In either event, the starfish has a strange way of ingesting the meal. It doesn't take the meal to its stomach; it takes its stomach to the meal by pushing its stomach outside its body, wrapping it around the meal and digesting it outside its body rather than inside. When the meal is finished, the stomach is swallowed again.

Sometimes the starfish get themselves organized into something of an army of invasion. A large group will descend in slow-motion movements and attack a big community of mussels.

This voracious appetite has made starfish one of the most dreaded and hated forms of sea life to oyster farmers, who can lose thousands of their charges in one sitting by a band of starfish.

Starfish come in a wide variety of sizes, shapes and colors. Some are so tiny they are hardly large enough to cover a 50-cent piece. Others, such as the stubby-legged slime star, have a protective device that protects them from other sea life. They secrete a thick mucus that is poisonous to fish. When the slime star is displayed in an aquarium, it must be displayed alone or its slime will kill the fish either by its toxic properties or by plugging the fishes' gills.

Other varieties have long, spindly arms that make them look as though they are suffering from malnutrition.

The basket star is perhaps the strangest of all. It has five arms, but branches similar to small bushes spring from each arm making them look something like a sea-going tumbleweed. It moves by undulating these arms and branches; and since it doesn't have suckers on its arms, it is believed to obtain its food by trapping small fish and other food in the branches or tendrils.

Unlike most forms of sea life with a tough skin, the starfish does not permit other sea life to cling to it, such as barnacles and algae. To keep itself cleared of these oceanic hitchhikers, starfish have hundreds of tiny, almost microscopic organs on their skin shaped something like pincers. These keep all living things off its skin.

Reproduction of starfish is not a carefully rehearsed event. They do not mate in any sense of the word, and simply cast their eggs and sperm into the water, letting fertilization occur by chance if at all.

However, a few species have females with strong mothering instincts. They not only carry their small in pouches near their mouths, they also protect the young until they are capable of protecting themselves. The average life span of most starfish is about four years. The purple starfish is an exception and is believed to live up to 20 years.

While they are best known as tidal zone creatures, starfish have been found in greater depths. Some have been dredged up from as deep as 19,000 feet.

SINCE only a small percentage of the population chooses to go among the sea life in scuba gear, most of us must be content to become acquainted with all the beautifully colored species of fish through photographs, films and aquariums. This group of gaily colored fish was photographed at the Sealife Park fish bowl on Oahu and gives only a suggestion of the wide variety of fish found in tropical waters.

Although the West Coast of America is dotted with the buoys scuba divers put up to mark their presence, it is the reefs off the Hawaiian Islands where the wealth of beautiful fish are found. On the Big Island of Hawaii are several firms operating out of resort areas that will instruct novices in scuba diving or simply snorkeling. The latter is a simpler form of recreation because all it requires is the ability to swim, a face mask and a breathing tube attached to the mask that permits you to spend hours cruising along on the surface peering in on the sea life from above. Most snorkelers wrap a water-ski safety belt around their waist so they can simply drift along without expending their energy staying afloat.

Scuba diving is a more complicated form of recreation and requires the use of air tanks, weights and other equipment. It is not something a novice should try without expert instruction. But its practitioners are quick to say it is worth the effort and expense because it puts you right in the midst of the sea life and away from the world of man, at least temporarily.

In many places along the Kona Coast of Hawaii, the shoreline is a series of shelves which end in dropoffs very abruptly because they were created by lava flows that came down to the sea and created steep underwater cliffs as the molten lava hit the cold water and hardened almost immediately. Thus, the tropical fish are forced to live in rather cramped areas.

The variety of fish in these narrow areas is astonishing. Some guide services provide each client with an identification sheet and often a slide show before the outing so they will know what kind of fish to expect.

One of the most interesting species, which invariably leads to joking among the clients, is the *hinalea,* which can change its sex "without going to a hospital and calling a press conference." Another is the *uhu,* which manufactures sand by scraping coral with its bony beak. Another is the *keke,* which inflates itself like a balloon to rise rapidly from danger.

The sea life along the West Coast is no less interesting, although the vivid colorations are often missing. Divers along the shores of Puget Sound frequently come face-to-face with an octopus, that shy and easily frightened creature that has been much maligned in horror stories and films. The largest octopuses in North America are often found in Puget Sound waters, as are the truly dangerous moray eels. These have a bite as strong as a steam shovel and are best observed from a distance. If they want to be left alone, it is wise to heed their wishes.

As noted earlier, many communities along the sheltered coves and bays have created artificial environments for underwater life by sinking old barges or dropping clusters of worn-out vehicle tires. Soon the sea life discovers these shelters, and urban areas for these creatures soon result.

Those sailors unfortunate enough to have to abandon ship and try to survive in small boats are almost always surprised at the lack of sea life in the middle of the ocean. It has often been referred to as an oceanic desert. Most of the sea life clings to the edges of the great oceans, somewhere between the continental shelf and the beach.

Beyond the continental shelf life becomes more and more scarce, in part because creatures, like plants, need sunlight to survive. A few species of sea life manage to survive in the very depths where virtually no sunlight penetrates, but these are only a tiny part of the life found along the shore.

FOR most of us, though, views of the surface of the sea with the shore in sight are sufficient. We can understand this relationship much better and feel more at ease in it than beneath the surface. This evening scene shows the effect of the low sun, breakers and an offshore wind that rips the top off waves as they come charging into shore. The average wave has been found to travel about 15 miles an hour, faster during a storm, slower in flat and calm weather. Still, the water itself doesn't move; it is energy that moves through the water. Even in the heaviest surf, if no wind is present, you can see the truth of this phenomenon by watching a stick in the water at the edge of the surf. It will move in relatively small concentric circles, rather than toward the beach, or be swept along in the slow current that moves along the shore.

SOMETIMES a photographer must move in almost nose-to-nose with the subject matter of the shoreline in order to show vividly the parts of the whole scene. Some refer to this as the "wet knee school of photography," meaning that the photographer gets down on his knees, and sometimes elbows, to capture a scene. This mass of seafoam bubbles creates a small galaxy of stars as the sunlight reflects off the bubbles. In a minute or so all that would remain here is bare and damp sand.

WHEN you go to the beach for socializing and the sand and people are more important than the sea, you may possibly be disappointed. But when you go to the sea and shore to experience and explore the interaction of land and water, the chances of your returning home without having a good time are remote. Some people say that watching sailboat races is no more exciting than watching paint dry. But those same people would never say that about something as simple as watching the waves come in, the tideline moving back and forth, and the shifting light patterns on the wave crests. One moment the offshore rocks are exposed with seaweed, barnacles and starfish clinging to them. An hour or less later everything may be covered with water, even in the trough between the waves. The seashore is always the same, yet always different. We tend to assign our own moods to it making it like an obscure poem whose meaning varies from reader to reader.

THE Na Pali Coast of Kauai is one of the wildest and most beautiful in the world. The mountains rise dramatically more than 4,000 feet straight up almost from the ocean floor. The sea comes crashing in against them, creating spectacular surfs. This coastline has been used as the setting of many South Pacific movies, and many parts of it have never been walked on by man. Not surprisingly, the ancient Hawaiians had many legends about the sea and shore and the gods, strong men and women and lesser mortals who frequented the coast. The Hawaiian Islands have a reputation—unearned—of being overdeveloped. Yet, it is impossible to drive entirely around three of the five developed islands, and Kauai is one of the least developed. Its residents do not permit high-rising buildings, and much of the island is still wild. Typically, the only island that does not permit visitors, the privately owned Niihau, is only a short distance off Kauai and peopled by nearly pure Hawaiians who still live there by choice.

LYING in the pounding surf like some beached creature of the sea, these offshore rocks take the first line of defense against the sea at Point Lobos State Reserve near Monterey, California. It was such scenery that inspired the poet, Robinson Jeffers, to write some of his most vivid and dramatic poetry during his tenure in a tower overlooking the sea. Jeffers' imagery ranged from the rocks that looked like boars' teeth to roots that looked like eagles' claws. Anyone who has read Jeffers' poetry cannot visit the Monterey and Carmel area without seeing some scenes in terms of his poetry.

SOMETIMES in beach scenery, as in art, the most simple scenes are the most dramatic and memorable. Here the main elements of the coast are shown in a straightforward manner—the sea, sky, land and plants—and we often come to associate this with the entire shoreline experience. It is the kind of simple and direct scenery we hope to capture on film, but often become so engrossed in enjoying it we forget to use the camera. There are many areas of the shoreline that give us a wide variety of scenery to enjoy without having to move more than a few feet. This scene at Ecola State Park in Oregon is a good example.

WHO can look at this scene and not be immediately reminded of a seashell or a musical instrument or . . . ? Although the exploding wave was photographed near Rampart Rock on the central Oregon Coast, similar explosive and beautiful wave formations are found all over the world when the surf comes in contact with the shore. Not captured on film, obviously, is the basso boom that comes from such events. Rather than being frightening, as from a roll of thunder or a bomb, there is something soothing about the so-called symphony of the surf.

IT is possible to spend hours and hours (the workaholics would say waste rather than spend) on the shore when such heavy surfs are coming in. These scenes, at Point Lobos and Shore Acres, make it easy to imagine the distant boom of the surf hitting one of the shoreline rocks, and the swirl and hiss of the surf churning over and around the dark stones that dissipate some of the energy expended by the sea against the shore. Sometimes such scenes are so hypnotic that it is best not to stop and watch if you have a later engagement; time has a way of slipping quickly by while watching such events.

THIS picturesque little cove in Boardman State Park in Oregon is composed of black lava sand, creating an entirely different set of colors and textures as the foamy surf washes in. Not far north of this beach, at the accurately named Gold Beach, a small gold rush occurred when flecks of gold were found in the sand that had been washed down the Rogue River. Similar gold rushes to beaches have occurred elsewhere—the most famous was on the beach off Nome, Alaska, in 1899. However, few of these gold rushes earn money for anyone other than proprietors of saloons, hotels and restaurants. Many types of machinery have been "invented" to extract gold from the beach sand, most depending on centrifugal force. Hardly anyone makes money on these machines except the inventor who sells shares in his doomed enterprise.

ONE of the best environmental study areas along the West Coast is the 50-odd mile long Oregon Coastal Dunes, where sand is steadily marching inland from the beach and engulfing the forest as it moves. The dunes vary from half a mile wide to five miles and have become a major tourist attraction. Motorized dune vehicles are permitted in some areas, and horses are available for riders to explore the area. The moving dunes have covered some lakes and threaten others. The area is of such importance for study and for recreation that a 32,000-acre Oregon Dunes National Recreation Area has been established between Florence and Coos Bay.

IN an effort to control the moving sand in some areas, beach grass has been planted to stabilize the sand as much as possible. Similar efforts have been made with success in other stretches of the Oregon Coast because once the sand begins moving inland, there is little else that will stop it. Conservationists have noted with some concern that the Sahara Desert is still growing and do not want a repeat of that along the Oregon Coast, even on a smaller and more localized scale.

AFTER suffering devastating fires caused by the over-population of gorse, a particularly hardy bush imported from Scotland, the Bandon area of Oregon has gradually been making a comeback with visitors. It is scenes such as this along the Bandon shoreline that make the area particularly attractive to people who like their scenery rugged. By the time visitors traveling south along the famed Highway 101 on Oregon's Coast have left Coos Bay and driven inland away from the sea, their next sighting of the surf is at Bandon. From here south into the northern California coastline the scenery is quite different than above Coos Bay. It is drier and the forests have thinned out, giving the seashore a more open and barren appearance.

SOME things are common to all stretches of beach throughout the world, things that man and his need for establishing territories cannot control. The surf continues to come in and out with the tides and storms, leaving behind small clusters of sparkling foam, depositing floating objects for us to ponder over and nurturing life both in and out of the water. The sea is one of those constants in the universe, and although it goes through subtle changes in its cycles of currents and amount of ice cap in the Arctic and Antarctic, these changes are part of the whole scheme of things that we can neither control nor totally understand.

Consequently we live with a vague fear of the ocean, as we do of the sun, because it is beyond our control. Thus, in an effort to appease these forces before they demolish mankind, some religions have been based on worshiping such natural forces in hopes that homage to them would offer protection from their immense and indiscriminate power.

Anything as familiar yet mysterious as the sea inevitably leads man to stretch his imagination and invent all sorts of monsters, imaginary kingdoms, nonexistent places and other things to fear. Some of the best adventure stories in the world literature have the sea as their basis. *Moby Dick* could have been written about a bear, but some of the great mystery of the novel would have been lacking. Even though we may not know Arctic regions as well as our own landscape, still we are more familiar with land. Also, man has always had a closer relationship with mammals of the land, while we still know very little about the lives of whales. Almost all scientific literature on sea mammals is laden with qualifying words and phrases such as "perhaps," "it is believed," "so far as we know" and other honest waffle-words.

Islands in the sea hold a greater fascination than most other land forms because they are remote—even those we can see from the shoreline—and because few of us have long-term experience with living on islands. Until the great influx of men and women from the temperate zones of Europe and America, the peoples living on these islands had centuries free of outside interference and were able to develop their own complex social and religious orders. Today only a few such island cultures have been able to remain intact; most have been either destroyed or severely altered by the newcomers with their technology and their insistence that their social and religious orders are superior.

One of the most touching such encounters between the technologically advanced Caucasians and island peoples came during that great social leveling event called World War II. Some Pacific islanders developed what is known as the cargo cults. These islanders, with virtually no previous contact with ships, planes, jeeps, and all the military tools and the various geegaws of our civilization, came to believe that all they needed to do in order to receive these things themselves was to build landing fields or boat docks, then sit and wait for their ship (or plane) to arrive with all the goods they had disgorged during the Pacific campaign of the war. How long it took these cargo cults to die out is anyone's guess, but one suspects there are still old men and women of the islands who occasionally look out to sea or into the sky for that great cargo to arrive.

This yearning for sudden wealth is constantly manifested in man's experience with the sea. Some people devote their entire adult lives to searching for sunken treasure. There persist beliefs, based on convincing artifacts, that various forms of treasure are buried along the West Coast and also in the Hawaiian Islands. Repeatedly, schemes are launched to extract gold or other precious metals from sand on the beach. We continue hoping and believing that somewhere beyond the horizon across the ocean is what we have been searching for all our lives. The sea presents a barrier between us and that promised land, and it is little wonder that many people, such as the ancient Greeks, believed that heaven lies somewhere out to sea.

THINGS that wash up on the beach after long sea voyages hold almost as much fascination for us as artifacts dug from dead cities of ancient civilizations. Even the debris from careless boaters, such as suntan-oil bottles and plastic oil containers, momentarily make us wonder where they were tossed overboard. Who among us hasn't hoped to find a bottle with a message sealed in it from someone on the opposite side of the ocean?

Books have been written about the manufacturing and markings of these glass floats from Japanese fishing vessels. As they become increasingly rare due to the use of other materials as fish-net floats, the value of such discoveries on beaches grows. Since much of their value is in the discovery, most beachcombers are content to take them home and use them as conversation pieces for years to come and would sell them only as a last resort against bankruptcy.

The sea produces some excellent home decorations, and many beach dwellers earn a decent income by picking up pieces of driftwood and turning them into conversation pieces. The combination of sea water, sun and sand often turns pieces of wood the color and texture of old pewter.

Consequently, on most mornings after storms blow away, the beaches attract strollers out in search of whatever the storm blew to shore. The most dedicated beachcombers will never hurry along the beach. Instead, they stroll slowly, poking into all the little coves and crawling over piles of logs and tree stumps in hopes of finding something the early arrivals might have missed. The first choice, of course, is these glass floats. But even when the outing yields nothing worth bringing home, the stroll is always a source of pleasure.

We tend to romanticize dedicated beachcombers almost as much as we did hoboes during the steam-railroad era. Many of us have spent some time yearning for the simple life of the beachcombers we have read about in romanticized versions of that way of life. We imagine ourselves cast up, either by accident or choice, on a remote island and having to live by our wits ala *Robinson Crusoe* until we are at last rescued. We think we could quickly build a house of driftwood and palm fronds, dig a well, find sufficient food from the trees and bushes and sea, and that we would become lean, tan and healthy. We would never be bored because we would be living in a land of tropical plenty with postcard-perfect sunrises, days filled with little adventures and nights around a fire eating our catch from the lagoon.

Factual accounts of such events don't hold up well against the romantic version. One man wrote of being delivered to an uninhabited tropical island and left for most of a day just for the experience. Although he knew he would be picked up before dark, he found himself totally bored before two hours had passed, and knew then that even if he could survive on an island, the monotony of the experience would be excruciating. In such circumstances, even a savage tropical storm would be welcome.

The West Coast of the United States is so heavily populated that there are few places where one would be lost more than a few days or a few hours, especially in California and most of Oregon. Only Washington has many miles of roadless and wild coastline remaining, and in the summers several backpackers pass every spot along the beach each day.

The Hawaiian Islands have many miles of shoreline remaining wild, especially on Kauai, Molokai, Lanai and parts of Maui. Those who have attempted to trek around these islands on the shoreline will confirm the suspicion that the romance of the situation quickly fades as the need for survival becomes apparent.

Consequently, most people from the temperate zones of Europe and North America who spend much time on remote islands are wealthy enough to come and go as they please and do not have to feel trapped any longer than they choose to. In the Hawaiian Islands they call it "island fever" when a newcomer begins feeling claustrophobic and says the islands are getting smaller and smaller.

EACH summer countless people arrive on the board and long beach at Cannon Beach in the lee of Haystack Rock to build sand castles and sand creatures as part of a competition. This form of recreation is probably one of the first man did on the seashore. Knowing that these creations will last only until the next high tide doesn't cause distress. They know their creations existed and take some pleasure in that knowledge, then go out at the next low tide and build more.

IN spite of our fears that have grown from the development of coastlines near major urban areas, a few wild places still remain that appear immune to shopping malls and neon lights. One such place is the Na Pali Coast of Kauai, shown here in the reds and yellows of evening as the sheer cliffs soar upward to more than 4,000 feet. This wild and rugged coastline can be reached by hiking a trail that leads from the end of the road. Or, helicopters operate on Kauai to fly visitors along the coast or up the famous Waimea Canyon, which rivals the Grand Canyon for magnificient erosion.

ALTHOUGH most people don't like to see a forest killed by the sea encroaching on land, such dramatic scenes have their own beauty. This garden of driftwood designs is at the foot of Cape Meares near Tillamook, Oregon, where the ocean and Tillamook River currents were altered by the construction of a jetty. Adding to the beauty is the autumn haze that mutes the shoreline in the distance. The drive from the town of Tillamook out to Cape Meares, then down past Cape Lookout and on to Cape Kiwanda, is one of the most beautiful drives in Oregon with the lighthouse at Cape Meares and the beautiful Cape Lookout State Park overlooking the ocean. Cape Kiwanda, of course, is the artistic stopover for photographers, painters and lovers of wild beauty.

WHEN Highway 101 was carved along the Oregon Coast, several headlands were cut off and isolated from the rest of the timbered coast. One was Cape Lookout, shown here with the sun penetrating the mists in the dense forest. In order to save such virgin headlands, the state created state parks or preserves. This one, barely penetrated by trails, is Cape Lookout State Park. As mentioned before, Cape Lookout is on the side road that leads west from Tillamook and ends at Cape Kiwanda. Here the highway engineers followed the path of least resistance from Tillamook and took Highway 101 inland through the dairy farms that have helped make Tillamook one of the cheese manufacturing centers of the West Coast.

LOOKING almost serpentine with its humps and curves, Twin Rocks is boldly outlined in the afternoon sun. The arch slowly grows larger and larger as the sea continues to erode away the stone. Sometime in the future, probably long after all of us are gone, the arch will crumble into the surf, leaving two separate sea stacks behind. Such scenes are common along coastlines throughout the world, particularly along the Pacific Rim. A few have been isolated inland as the currents along the shore shift and deposit sand that slowly extends that stretch of beach out toward the sea. Although these shifts in currents and eddies sometimes occur naturally, most result from some activity by man, such as building a jetty or breakwater along a river mouth.

WE envy birds their apparent freedom and their ability to be almost equally at ease on the water, on land and most of all in the air. Many people who feel confined by their roles in life often dream of flying or swooping and soaring high above the earth, one step further than those who accomplish the same with sailplanes and the more flimsy craft some use that is more of a kite than an airplane. So birds fascinate us, and some people spend the years following retirement traveling the continent, or even the world, "birding," watching birds and trying to identify as many species as possible. Here a shorebird ignores the people nearby to go about its search for food on California's Monterey Peninsula.

BECAUSE of this fascination with birds, nearly all the offshore rocks along the West Coast are dedicated bird refuges, and it is a federal crime to climb around on these rocks so designated. The Audubon Society, a national organization with chapters in nearly every part of the country, frequently sponsors field trips with members and potential members—one of the best ways to learn the fascinating hobby of birdwatching. Sometimes the best way to approach is in full sight of the birds instead of attempting to stalk them. Apparently part of the birds' protective instincts is to avoid any creature that tries to approach them in a stealthy, stalking manner. Migration and nesting periods are the best times with the peak spring period in April and May. The fall migration period is from August through September, although it can begin a bit earlier and extend into October, depending on what the birds' instincts tell them about the coming winter.

OBVIOUSLY the sun sets every day of every year and every century and is always colorful if it is in sight during those last few minutes. But we never tire of watching this event that is both mundane and remarkable. We expect each one to be more beautiful, more dramatic and more emotionally moving than the last, and somehow we are seldom disappointed. This sunset occurred at the Point Reyes National Seashore Park just north of San Francisco.

YET each sunset is worth the wait. Some visitors to the shoreline return inland and say they seemed to have spent more time watching sunsets than anything else. If sunsets didn't invoke such a strong response in nearly everyone, they wouldn't be so popular for magazine covers, posters, business advertisements and a host of other uses. This scene, taken on the Monterey Coast of California, has the added ingredient of a rain squall far out to sea that gives an additional element to the scene.

THIS picturesque old tree in the San Juan Islands of Washington has survived storms and undercutting that makes it almost horizontal. Another sunset means the same to it that sunsets mean to man: one more day of life that it has survived. Since the sky of the Northwest is so often overcast, sunsets with such dramatic colors aren't as common as in southern Oregon, California and Hawaii. Consequently, sunsets, like clear days when all the mountains around Puget Sound can be seen, are observed with rapt intensity and appreciation by residents and visitors.

THE most dramatic landmark at Cannon Beach, Oregon, is the gigantic monolith called Haystack Rock, standing only a short distance offshore and accessible during low-tide periods. Thus, it is almost natural that the smaller and more slender offshore rocks be called The Needles. Although shown here silhouetted against a sunset, they look more blunt than most needles. This area of sand and stone and tide pools is used nearly every summer by groups of biology and oceanography students as a workshop.

ALTHOUGH most lighthouses are automated today and operate the clock around instead of being turned off between dawn and dusk, still we associate lighthouses with the lonely hours after the evening meal and all through the night. It wasn't too many years ago that each lighthouse was manned, and there have always been more along the Oregon Coast than the other two states on the Pacific. This one, however, is on the Washington side of the Columbia River at North Head, where it has helped guide seamen into the Columbia for decades.

The most dramatic of the lighthouses is between Seaside and Cannon Beach, Oregon. This is the famous Tillamook Lighthouse that was manned for decades before it, too, was automated. Lives were lost trying to build it. It was one of the worst places for lighthouse keepers to be stationed because each time the supply ship came to give the men a few days ashore, it was more adventure than most men wanted just to get on and off the solitary rock. They were transported between ship and rock on breeches buoys. If the seas were high, as they frequently are in the area, the men swayed up and down, sometimes getting a dunking before they reached the ship or rock.

Life in the lighthouse was as comfortable as the Coast Guard could make it, but there was nothing anyone could do to ease the strain of sitting out a severe storm when the sea picked up rocks and smashed them into living quarters.

Eventually the lighthouse was abandoned and an automated beacon placed on a nearby rock. The lighthouse was declared surplus and available for private ownership.

It is along the shore that we are made most conscious that all the elements of land, sea and sky are so closely related and that everything but those three elements are of little significance, including man. It is good for us to stand on the edge of the sea and realize that the sea is not affected by our presence or our absence, that it was here long before any creature crawled out of it to breathe the air without having to filter oxygen out of saltwater. It helps us keep our perspective about the planet—and ourselves.

Index

L

M

N

P

R